EDWARD VII

Prince Edward, *c.*1875.
(Camera Press, London; photograph by Bassano, G56)

EDWARD VII

Image of an Era
1841 - 1910

Dana Bentley-Cranch

Published in association with
the National Portrait Gallery

London HMSO

ISBN 0 11 290508 0

Designed by HMSO Graphic Design

British Library Cataloguing in Publication Data
A CIP catalogue record for this book
is available from the British Library

HMSO

HMSO publications are available from:

HMSO Publications Centre
(Mail, fax and telephone orders only)
PO Box 276, London, SW8 5DT
Telephone orders 071-873 9090
General enquiries 071-873 0011
(queuing system in operation for both numbers)
Fax orders 071-873 8200

HMSO Bookshops
49 High Holborn, London, WC1V 6HB
(counter service only)
071-873 0011   Fax 071-873 8200
258 Broad Street, Birmingham, B1 2HE
021-643 3740   Fax 021-643 6510
Southey House, 33 Wine Street, Bristol, BS1 2BQ
0272-264306   Fax 0272 294515
9–21 Princess Street, Manchester, M60 8AS
061-834 7201   Fax 061-833 0634
16 Arthur Street, Belfast, BT1 4GD
0232-238451   Fax 0232 235401
71 Lothian Road, Edinburgh, EH3 9AZ
031-228 4181   Fax 031-229 2734

HMSO's Accredited Agents
(see Yellow Pages)
and through good booksellers

Printed in the UK for HMSO
Dd 294222   C50   9/92

CONTENTS

ACKNOWLEDGEMENTS

*A*CKNOWLEDGEMENTS are due to the following, for permission to quote from written material: Punch Publications to quote the lines 'Huzza! we've a little prince at last, A Roaring Royal Boy!', from the 13 November 1841 issue of *Punch*, on pp vii, 1 and 152 of this book; David Higham Associates Ltd, for the song from Sir Osbert Sitwell's *Great Morning* (Macmillan, 1948) on p 157; Penguin Books Ltd for the Coronation song from *The Edwardians* by J B Priestley, (Heinemann/Rainbird, 1970, p 26, copyright © J B Priestley, 1970) on p 125; Longman Group UK for material from H Bolitho, *A Biographer's Notebook*, Longman, 1950, used in chapter 3 (we have been unable to trace the copyright holder of this book and would be grateful for any information which would enable us to do so); and to Lady de Bellaigue, Registrar, for permission to quote material from the Royal Archives.

The author wishes to thank Mr Philip Glover, Mr Gavin Turner and Ms Ruth Bowden of HMSO; Mr John Adamson and Mr K K Yung of the National Portrait Gallery; Mr Terence Pepper of the National Portrait Gallery Archives; Professor C A Mayer; Dr Rosalind K Marshall; Mrs Nan Marshall; Mr Rudi Jagersbacher of the Langham Hilton in London; the Director of the Hôtel du Palais in Biarritz and the staff at Canada House (Canadian High Commission) in London for their much appreciated collaboration.

Edward's christening in St George's Chapel, Windsor, by Sir George Hayter. (Royal Collection, St James's Palace. © Her Majesty The Queen)

1
SON OF VICTORIA

'NEVER MIND, the next will be a Prince!' Queen Victoria's confident prediction after the birth of her first child – a daughter – was fulfilled a year later. The future Edward VII was born at Buckingham Palace twelve minutes before eleven o'clock on the morning of 9 November 1841. To the young Queen and her husband, Prince Albert, both aged twenty-two, the arrival of this son and heir completed their domestic happiness. To the Queen's subjects it signalled an outburst of popular joy with bells pealing across the country, toasts being drunk and the newly founded *Punch* magazine excitedly telling its readers: 'Huzza! we've a little Prince at last, A Roaring Royal Boy!' The baby was healthy and handsome, as his proud mother noted: 'our little Boy is a wonderfully large and strong child with very large dark-blue eyes and a pretty little mouth'.

'The Boy', as his parents called him during the first months of his life, assumed at birth an impressive array of hereditary titles: Duke of Cornwall, Duke of Rothesay, Earl of Carrick, Baron of Renfrew, Lord of the Isles and Great Steward of Scotland. His mother created him Prince of Wales – the title by which he was known for fifty-nine years – and Earl of Chester, and chose for him the names 'Albert' ('Bertie' to the family) and 'Edward' (his selected designation when King). Edward's Christening, which took place on 25 January 1842 at St George's Chapel, Windsor, was a grand affair. Two archbishops and four bishops performed the ceremony, the Duke of Wellington carried the Sword of State, the Duchess of Buccleuch carried the baby to the font, the King of Prussia was present as godfather, Handel's 'Hallelujah Chorus' rang out and 'The Boy' behaved splendidly.

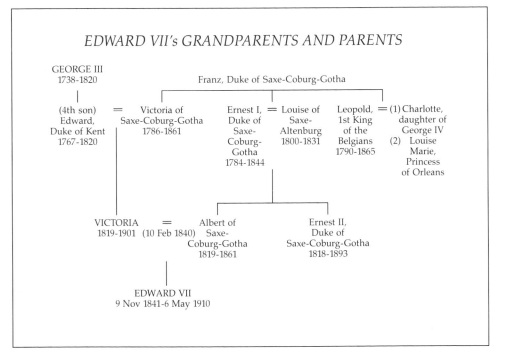

EDWARD VII's GRANDPARENTS AND PARENTS

GEORGE III
1738-1820

Franz, Duke of Saxe-Coburg-Gotha

(4th son) = Victoria of
Edward, Saxe-Coburg-Gotha
Duke of Kent 1786-1861
1767-1820

Ernest I, = Louise of
Duke of Saxe-
Saxe- Altenburg
Coburg- 1800-1831
Gotha
1784-1844

Leopold, = (1) Charlotte,
1st King daughter of
of the George IV
Belgians (2) Louise
1790-1865 Marie,
Princess
of Orleans

VICTORIA = Albert of
1819-1901 (10 Feb 1840) Saxe-
Coburg-Gotha
1819-1861

Ernest II,
Duke of
Saxe-Coburg-Gotha
1818-1893

EDWARD VII
9 Nov 1841-6 May 1910

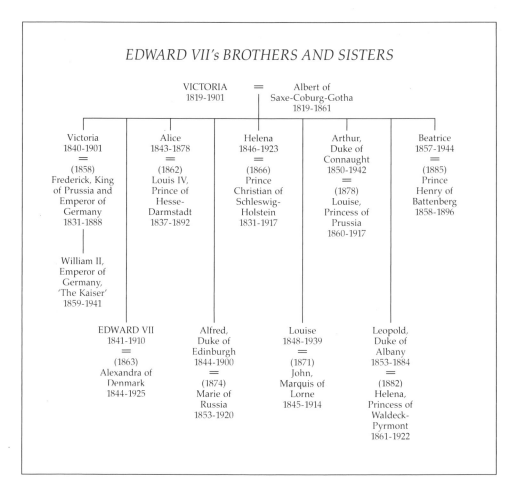

EDWARD VII's BROTHERS AND SISTERS

VICTORIA
1819-1901
=
Albert of
Saxe-Coburg-Gotha
1819-1861

| Victoria 1840-1901 = (1858) Frederick, King of Prussia and Emperor of Germany 1831-1888 | Alice 1843-1878 = (1862) Louis IV, Prince of Hesse-Darmstadt 1837-1892 | Helena 1846-1923 = (1866) Prince Christian of Schleswig-Holstein 1831-1917 | Arthur, Duke of Connaught 1850-1942 = (1878) Louise, Princess of Prussia 1860-1917 | Beatrice 1857-1944 = (1885) Prince Henry of Battenberg 1858-1896 |

William II,
Emperor of
Germany,
'The Kaiser'
1859-1941

| EDWARD VII 1841-1910 = (1863) Alexandra of Denmark 1844-1925 | Alfred, Duke of Edinburgh 1844-1900 = (1874) Marie of Russia 1853-1920 | Louise 1848-1939 = (1871) John, Marquis of Lorne 1845-1914 | Leopold, Duke of Albany 1853-1884 = (1882) Helena, Princess of Waldeck-Pyrmont 1861-1922 |

A Highland jacket and kilt (left) and plaid satin dress (right) worn by little Edward, c.1844–5.
(Museum of London)

Edward standing beside his mother to receive Coldstream Guardsmen returning wounded from the Crimean War, 1856.
(Windsor Castle, Royal Library. © Her Majesty The Queen)

But the early glow of parental approval was soon to fade. Victoria and Albert, determined to produce a perfect occupant of the throne, drew up, after earnest consultations with many experts including a phrenologist, a stringent educational programme for their small son. From the age of seven the young Prince was placed under the supervision of tutors and subjected to a rigorous timetable of lessons; daily reports to his anxious parents became a gloomy chronicle of failures, tantrums and exhausting scenes. 'All work and no play' did not make Edward a dull boy, but it turned his childhood into an uneasy and frustrating period. The long days of lessons were unrelieved by any association with boys of his own age. Although the royal nursery filled up rapidly – by 1857 Victoria had nine children – and the heir thus found himself a member of a large family, he was kept strictly away from what his parents feared might be 'contaminating' outside influences. For a boy who from his earliest days displayed an affectionate nature, a marked tendency for companionship and a loyalty in friendship – attributes which he kept throughout his life – the lack of young friends was a grievous deprivation. Family outings to the pantomime and theatre, or public appearances with his parents, did not do much to lessen the Prince's sense of isolation or help him to overcome his feelings of inferiority. He was certainly a reluctant scholar, but when he finally emerged from the schoolroom his attainments, paradoxically enough, were precisely those which were to stand him in good stead throughout his career as heir-in-waiting and as monarch, namely exceptional powers of observation and an astonishingly retentive memory. To these should be added his linguistic abilities; at the age of five little Edward was speaking and reading German, and fluency in French soon followed.

The parents' critical attitude to what they considered their son's shortcomings was not shared by other observers. Henry Ponsonby, on being appointed as Equerry to Albert, met Edward in 1857 and described him as very lively and

3

pleasant and one of the nicest boys he had ever seen, and in the following year the politician Benjamin Disraeli, an experienced and perceptive judge of character who later became Edward's friend, thought him informed, intelligent and with a particularly sweet manner. The uneasy relations between Edward and his parents haunted the remaining years of his boyhood. While Victoria had to admit that his heart was 'good, warm and affectionate', she also considered him 'idle and weak'. Albert, who made his son keep a diary and insisted on reading it, constantly deplored its meagre and childish contents and sternly demanded not merely bare facts but 'impressions of things'. By the time the Prince reached fifteen years of age, however, although the bookish education and rigid control of conduct – and the parental misgivings – were still intact, Albert had yielded to experts' advice to introduce some minor alleviations to the regime. These included permission for Edward to choose his own food – subject to consultation with doctors – and to select small articles of dress such as hats and ties. A year later this permission was extended to cover the choice of his entire wardrobe, although not without a moralising admonition from his mother: 'we do expect that you will never wear anything *extravagant* or *slang*, not because we don't like it, but because it would prove a want of self-respect and be an offence against decency, leading – as it has often done in others – to an indifference to what is morally wrong'. Moral guidance figured largely in the educational process of the heir. Victoria's worried observation on his sixteenth birthday, 'may God bless him and help him and us through the difficult task of education. It is such an anxiety to us', ushered in a long period of preparing the Prince for his Confirmation in the Church of England. At its conclusion Edward was given an hour-long examination in the presence of his critical parents by Gerald Wellesley, Dean of Windsor, and passed it successfully. On the following day, 1 April 1858, with the Prince, according to his mother, in a gentle, good and proper state of mind, the Confirmation Ceremony was performed by the Archbishop of Canterbury and Bishop Wilberforce of Oxford in St George's Chapel, Windsor, before a large assembly which included all the leading politicians.

By this time the education of the heir to the throne was provoking widespread discussion. Not since 1762 had an heir been born to a reigning monarch, and from Edward's birth the whole country had displayed a proprietary interest in their future King. Much advice, and criticism, was increasingly directed at Albert. Edward himself had only one desire, to escape from 'book-learning' and join the army. This ambition dismayed his parents, who had to explain to their disappointed son that, as heir to the throne, he belonged, as it were, not only to the whole country and its overseas possessions, but also to both the armed services, and therefore could not pursue a career in one branch alone. His disappointment was somewhat tempered by a parental plan to allow him, if not to serve in the army, at least, as they put it, 'to learn in it'. This plan took the form of removing the Prince from the distractions of Court life and settling him, with an entourage of three specially selected equerries, his tutors and chaplain, in a separate household, the White Lodge in Richmond Park, for a few months, during which time preparation for a military entrance examination would be added to his other studies. But the independence which this move appeared to envisage was illusionary. The three equerries were instructed by Albert, to whom they had to report, to supervise very closely every aspect of his son's behaviour; there was to be no 'slouching' or 'careless self-indulgent lounging' or 'lolling in

4

Edward (far right) on the terrace at Osborne House, Isle of Wight, with his family in 1857. Other members of the family (left to right): Alfred, Prince Albert, Helena, Arthur, Alice, Queen Victoria holding baby Beatrice, Victoria, Louise and Leopold. (National Portrait Gallery, London; photograph by L Caldesi)

armchairs or sofas', no 'dandyism' in apparel, no gossip, cards or billiards, and definitely no 'practical jokes'. Edward was to be encouraged to spend any spare time left over from his studies in reading 'good books and plays'. Life at the White Lodge was thus little different from that in the schoolroom and stiflingly dull for a seventeen-year-old. Even the occasional dinner parties the heir was instructed to give were exclusively for famous men and worthy members of society selected by his parents. That the middle-aged and elderly guests invariably enjoyed these dinners must be attributed to the good manners with which their young host concealed his inevitable boredom.

The Prince's seventeenth birthday on 9 November 1858 ushered in his eighteenth year, at the end of which he could legally, if the necessity arose, ascend to the throne. His solicitous mother, who had herself become Queen at that age, and his indefatigable father marked the occasion by sending a long memorandum which set out a strict code of conduct for the young man: he should learn to organise his own time and utilise it in the best possible manner, he should make himself as independent as possible of the services of his servants and he should always remember that life is composed of duties which a true gentleman performs cheerfully. To these rather quelling strictures were appended the more cheerful riders that his annual allowance was to be increased to £500, that he was to receive the Knighthood of the Garter and that he was gazetted Lieutenant-Colonel in the Grenadier Guards. This latter announcement had the Prince donning his uniform and repairing immediately to the Horse Guards to report to his superior officer. Another change marking the beginning of this important year was that Edward's tutor was retired and his place taken by a 'Governor', a new post created by Albert. The man appointed to this key position was Colonel Bruce, brother of the Earl of Elgin and an officer in the Guards with diplomatic and cultural experience. The dignified title notwithstanding, the role of the Governor was intended to be very similar to that of the erstwhile tutor. His instructions, handed to him by the Queen on the Prince's birthday, dealt fully with his responsibilities and duties. He was to 'stand in' as a parent in fact, assume full control of his charge, to regulate his movements, the employment of his time, all the minute details of his daily life, to fix regular hours every day for his studies, to encourage him in habits of reflection and self-denial and in the conscientious discharge of his duties towards God and man, and to send in full reports on every aspect to the parents. Edward thus faced, in spite of his new status, the prospect of another long and daunting period of tutelage. He had not given up the idea of a military career, and pleaded to be allowed to undergo military training at Aldershot. But this time not only his parents but his Governor as well were strongly opposed to the idea, Colonel Bruce in particular dwelling on the temptations and unsuitable companions which he considered insepar-able from military life.

It was decided that an 'educational tour' was just what the Prince needed and that the destination should be Rome, a city where art past and present flourished, where architecture could be profitably studied and where some grounding in international politics and culture could be acquired. Before the trip began many experts were consulted as to what the Prince should be shown, and how his artistic propensities should be stimulated. On being applied to, the writer and art critic John Ruskin gave the somewhat unhelpful answer that the young man should not regard art only as a vehicle of luxury and pride, that he should form his own opinions and that one of the duties of

John Ruskin (1819–1900), author and critic. (National Portrait Gallery, London; photograph by T A and J Green, 1885)

monarchs was to preserve monuments which would otherwise crumble away.

On 10 January 1859 the party set off, travelling via Brussels and German towns, the Brenner pass and Verona, paying calls and sightseeing on the way and reaching Rome on 4 February. Edward's entourage included his Governor and Mrs Bruce, his classics tutor, Mr Tarver, and Mrs Tarver, his equerries, chaplain and doctor. Once established in the Hôtel d'Angleterre, the young man had to settle down, somewhat reluctantly, to the customary regime of study: preparation before breakfast, an Italian lesson from ten o'clock to eleven o'clock, reading with Mr Tarver from eleven o'clock to mid-day, translating French from five o'clock to six o'clock, and private reading and music from six o'clock to seven o'clock. The afternoons were spent in visiting monuments, museums, churches and artists' studios. Reports from the Governor on his charge's progress, or lack of it, proliferated to the critical parents at home who were haunted by the irrational fear that the monarchy would be doomed should their son have to succeed at an early age (Victoria, who lived to the age of eighty-one, was convinced that she would die young). Edward was castigated as being incurably lazy, interested only in dress, ceremonials and other frivolities, and his diary, sent home in instalments, came in for the usual disparaging comments from his father – it was too brief, too stilted, not enough serious reflections and so on.

But this reproving and critical attitude was not shared by the many visitors to Rome who met the young Prince. The city was a fashionable winter residence and the home of many artists and writers. The educational afternoon outings included a visit to the studio of Edward Lear, the artist and author of the *'Nonsense'* books who had met the four-year-old Edward in the summer of 1846 when giving Victoria a course of drawing lessons. Lear gives an amusing account of preparing for the Prince's visit. On 29 March at three o'clock a note arrived from Colonel Bruce asking if four o'clock would be convenient. Lear

Edward Lear (1812–1888), artist and writer.
(National Portrait Gallery, London;
photograph by McLean, Melhuish and Haes)

John Lothrop Motley (1814–1877), American historian and diplomat. (National Portrait Gallery, London; photograph by John Watkins)

and his servant immediately rushed round the studio trying to get it cleaned up, the servant was hustled into his Sunday suit, and in a state of agitation Lear positioned himself on the landing to be ready to greet the party. But in spite of this nervous beginning the visit was a great success. Edward's good manners and intelligent comments charmed the artist, who showed his young guest a large selection of his work – his sketches, Greek pictures and oil-paintings of Palestine. When asked if he were tired of seeing so many, the Prince eagerly denied it, and Lear proudly recorded that the visit had lasted for over an hour.

Another visitor to Rome, the distinguished American historian and diplomat John Lothrop Motley, was invited to one of the dinner parties given by Edward in his hotel, and wrote home an appreciative account to his mother. Disarmingly declaring that this honour had been quite unexpected, he described how Colonel Bruce paid a call on him to invite him and how he found himself one of a small intimate party of nine. At dinner Motley sat on one side of Mrs Bruce, the Prince on the other, and round the small table the talk was general. After dinner Edward asked the American to sit beside him and they conversed together on German literature, Goethe and Schiller and objects of art in Rome. The historian described his young host's pure, healthy and fresh complexion, short-cut light-brown hair, large blue eyes, frank expression, ready and genuine smile and his extremely good manners. Motley summed up his impressions: 'Altogether the dinner was a very pleasant one, and it was very agreeable to me to have made the acquaintance of the future Sovereign of the magnificent British Empire in such a simple and unceremonious manner. I have not had much to do with Royal personages, but of those I have known, I know none whose address is more winning, and with whom one feels more at one's ease.' Another dinner guest to be impressed by Edward was Robert Browning; the poet described his host as a gentle, refined boy, who spoke little but listened attentively to the conversation. The Prince, therefore, even at the young age of seventeen, would appear to have discovered, without being taught, the art of being a good host, namely, the

Little Edward in sailor costume, by Franz Xaver Winterhalter, 1846.
(Royal Collection, St James's Palace. © Her Majesty The Queen)

Queen Victoria (1819–1901) by Sir George Hayter. An 1863 replica of the 1838 original.
(National Portrait Gallery, London)

Albert (1819–1861), Prince Consort to Queen Victoria, by Franz Xaver Winterhalter. An 1867
replica of the 1859 original.
(National Portrait Gallery, London)

Edward, Duke of Kent,
Victoria's father. Painting
by Sir William Beechey,
1818.
(National Portrait Gallery,
London)

Victoria, Duchess of Kent,
Victoria's mother.
Painting by Franz Xaver
Winterhalter (reduced
version, 1857).
(National Portrait Gallery,
London)

Duke Ernest I of Saxe-Coburg-Gotha, Albert's father. Painting by George Dauve, 1819, Ehrenburg Palace, Coburg.
(Bayerische Verwaltung der staatlichen Schlösser, Gärten und Seen. Coburger Landesstiftung)

Duchess Louise, Albert's mother. Painting by Ebart, c.1900 (from an earlier model), Rosenau Palace near Coburg.
(Bayerische Verwaltung der staatlichen Schlösser, Gärten und Seen. Coburger Landesstiftung)

Edward in 1858, pastel by George Richmond.
(National Portrait Gallery, London)

14

Robert Browning (1812–1889), poet, who met young Prince Edward in Rome in 1859. Portrait by Michele Gordigiani, 1858. (National Portrait Gallery, London)

Professor Lyon Playfair (1818–1898), 1st Baron, the scientist who taught Edward in Edinburgh and became his lifelong friend. Enamel miniature by John Haslem, 1854. (National Portrait Gallery, London)

King Leopold I of the Belgians (1790–1865), Edward's great-uncle. Miniature on ivory by an unknown artist, 1815.
(National Portrait Gallery, London)

King Leopold's Palace at Laeken, where Edward and Alexandra became engaged.
(Inbel, Brussels)

Frederic Leighton (1830–1896), painter, photographed in costume, by David Wilkie Wynfield in the 1860s. (National Portrait Gallery, London)

ability to create a pleasant and easy atmosphere and to encourage his guests to converse, an achievement which, while apparent to others, remained unappreciated by his Governor and parents.

The programme of study and visits continued during the stay in Rome. One of the studios inspected was that of Frederic (later Lord) Leighton, then a young painter aged under thirty. Edward wrote about three pictures he had seen there of a beautiful Roman woman, each depicting her in a different attitude, and later he purchased one of Leighton's pictures, the much-admired *Nanna*. For his part Leighton reported happily to his mother that the Prince and his party had said they liked his studio better than any other they had seen. The painter was also a dinner party guest, and his acquaintance with Edward, begun in Rome, lasted throughout his life.

The political situation in Italy cut short the Prince's 'educational visit' to Rome and cancelled his projected tour of the northern Italian cities and a proposed study period in Geneva. The outbreak of hostilities, which had long been threatened and which eventually led to the unification and independence of Italy, began with a declaration of war by the Emperor of Austria on the King of Sardinia at the end of April. Albert telegraphed urgent instructions to the royal party to embark at once and sail for Gibraltar. Edward duly noted in his diary how sad he was to leave Rome where his stay had been agreeable and (he added dutifully) instructive. Transferring to the Royal Yacht at Gibraltar, the party cruised around, visiting Spain and Portugal, paying calls on family and friends, and finally reaching home at the end of June 1859.

The Prince was greeted with the customary parental strictures and reproofs – his diary was adjudged to be meagre and showing little evidence of mental acquirements – and new plans of study were outlined. Edward, still begging to be allowed to pursue his heart's desire, a military career at Aldershot, was told that instead he would have to go to university, attending in turn both Oxford and Cambridge, and that the summer months would have to be spent in Edinburgh in a preparatory 'cramming' programme to fit him for academic life. The reluctant Prince, accompanied by his Governor and Mr Tarver, was accordingly packed off to reside in Holyroodhouse. His studies included Greek and Roman history, Italian, French and German. But a preliminary course in applied science, to be taught by the holder of the Chair of Chemistry in the University of Edinburgh, Professor Lyon Playfair, proved a welcome addition to the regime, and resulted in a long friendship between pupil and teacher. Playfair devised laboratory experiments to attract, and retain, the Prince's interest. One of these led to a dramatic demonstration: asked by the Professor if he had faith in science, Edward replied that he certainly had; his hand was then thoroughly washed with ammonia by Playfair and he was requested to place it in a cauldron of lead boiling at white heat and ladle out a portion. 'Do you ask me to do this?' asked the amazed young man. 'I do,' was the firm reply, upon which Edward instantly complied, emerging unscathed and triumphant from this test of courage and nerve, and with an enhanced interest in science. Perhaps because of the sympathetic approach of Playfair and other experienced teachers, the Edinburgh 'cramming' programme, which had provoked much public pity for the hapless heir, proved successful. When Albert arrived in Edinburgh in September to conduct an investigation into the summer's work, he was pleasantly surprised at the favourable reports of his son's tutors. Edward was allowed a short break at Balmoral which he spent in strenuous hill climbing and shooting, claiming two fine stags, before arriving in Oxford on 17 October to begin his university career.

The life of an undergraduate is normally associated with a measure of freedom, especially from parental control, but such was not to be the case for the heir. Albert, prophesying endless difficulties if his son were to mingle freely with a multitude of young men and form friendships, insisted that, although Edward's college would be Christ Church, he must not go into residence there. A nearby house, Frewin Hall, was rented, and the Prince's household set up there under the control of the Governor and with the usual entourage. The Prince was thus excluded from most university and college activities; his studies were conducted privately with a few carefully selected companions, by equally carefully chosen tutors and closely supervised by Albert during his frequent visits. But even in these secluded and unpromising conditions Edward managed to impress and to form some lasting relationships. Dean Lidell, Head of Christ Church, found him one of the nicest and most modest of young men, noting approvingly that he possessed the royal faculty of never forgetting a face, and Edward kept up a friendly correspondence with Mrs Lidell for years. Dr Arthur Stanley, Professor of Ecclesiastical History and later Dean of Westminster, who was entrusted with the Prince's religious teaching, later became one of his travelling companions. Some small relief from studies took the form of the heir hosting dinner parties, as he had done in Rome, at Frewin Hall, and having an occasional outing on the hunting field – a sport of which his parents did not greatly approve – with Lord Macclesfield's South Oxfordshire pack.

On 9 November 1859 the Prince celebrated his eighteenth birthday, a historic occasion in that it marked his royal 'coming-of-age'. But his emancipation was still a little way off; not until the following summer was he to experience a taste of freedom and come of age as a 'public image' in the exhilarating surroundings of the New World.

Edward as an undergraduate at Oxford University, 1860. He joined the University in the –
long obsolete – grade of 'nobleman'. Undergraduates thus classified were entitled to a
gold-tasselled cap, which the Prince appears to be wearing in this photograph by Hills and
Saunders.
(National Portrait Gallery, London)

2

INTO A NEW WORLD

*T*HE IDEA of a royal visit to Canada had been mooted since the end of the Crimean War in 1856. Canada, which had equipped and sent an infantry regiment to fight alongside Britain in that conflict, subsequently invited Queen Victoria to pay a visit to the colony. She declined, promising however to send the Prince of Wales in her place when he was old enough, and in 1860 this promise was fulfilled. Albert, Victoria and the Government decided to send Edward during the Oxford University summer vacation, and preparations were soon under way. The heir was to participate in two important public ceremonies: the opening of the railway bridge across the St Lawrence river at Montreal, and the laying of a cornerstone at the Parliament House at Ottawa, the new capital of the United Canadas, as well as representing the Queen on an extended tour across the country. These exciting plans aroused the interest of the United States and resulted in invitations for the Prince to include America in his itinerary and, among other engagements, to spend a few days with President Buchanan at the White House and to visit New York. After much political deliberation Victoria and her Ministers agreed to this extension with certain conditions: in Canada Edward was to act as the Queen's deputy, while the visit to America was to be a private one. He was to travel as a student – studying 'American life' – and, except in Washington, was to be put up in private hotels.

Edward, all eagerness to embark on this adventure, agreed to everything. His suite was carefully chosen to include the Duke of Newcastle, Secretary of State for the Colonies, Governor Bruce, now promoted to General, equerries and a doctor. An innovation which strikes a modern note was the addition to the party of a journalist and an artist who together sent home detailed descriptions of what was to prove a triumphantly successful trip. A special photograph of the Prince was issued to mark the occasion, and on 9 July 1860 the party sailed from Southampton on the man-of-war HMS *Hero*, accompanied by the escort ships *Ariadne* and *Nile*. Edward was lodged on the upper quarter-deck of the *Hero* in the accommodation usually reserved for the captain. In the small sleeping cabin his cot was slung for him every night; a speaking-tube enabled him to summon his servant. The comfortable little sitting room held a table and two small sofas (these inducements for 'lounging' and 'lolling' must have escaped the parental eye) and led into the dining room. This handsome apartment with space for twenty-two chairs around the mahogany table contained, as well as an engraving of Lord Nelson, mementoes of the famous Admiral in the shape of four long silver lantern-like candle holders from the *Victory*. Here Edward took his meals, breakfast about nine o'clock, luncheon at one o'clock and, at five o'clock, dinner to which he always invited one or more of the ship's officers. His guests often included the young midshipmen whose company the Prince, surrounded by his usual entourage of middle-aged and elderly men, particularly appreciated. During the two weeks of the voyage he was coached by his Governor and the Duke in details of all the places on his tour, the addresses to which he would have to reply and the political implications of his visit. Cheerfully receiving all this instruction, he still found time to enjoy the voyage, to be lively and sociable and to indulge in a little 'sky-larking' when sitting cross-legged on the upper deck with his telescope in his hand, signalling the other ships in the escort and sending humorous messages.

Hero made good time and docked on 23 July, two days ahead of schedule, at St John's on Newfoundland. Here the Prince, staying at Government House, made his first public appearance and experienced the enthusiastic welcome which was to be repeated at every stage of his visit. The town was crammed with about three-quarters of the population of the whole island to watch the royal visitor inspect a force of newly enlisted Volunteers – a new scheme of military defence, recently started in England, which Edward had been requested to encourage in Canada – and receive fourteen Loyal Addresses. To these he read replies, clearly and without nervousness, as the Duke of Newcastle reported back to the Queen, commending at the same time his frank and friendly manners. General Bruce added a somewhat sour comment that the Prince seemed pleased with everything, including himself, but even that stern critic had to admit that his charge had acquitted himself admirably. A surprise present came in the form of a huge black Newfoundland dog wearing a great silver collar around his neck. Edward delighted his audience by declaring that he had just been wishing for such a dog on the voyage and by deciding to call his new pet 'Cabot' after the discoverer of Newfoundland. Cabot was safely installed on *Hero* and eventually made his way to England. (His proud owner later related how, when Cabot first landed, he was immediately bitten by another dog but was able to retaliate and killed his attacker 'off hand'!)

The royal party re-embarked and sailed on to Cape Breton Island, landing at Sydney Harbour to visit an Indian Camp and to inspect another contingent of Volunteers. On 26 July *Hero* reached Nova Scotia and Edward landed at Halifax. The town, bedecked with flags, gay with huge triumphal arches and full of excited crowds, had been eagerly anticipating the visit. According to

Edward holding a levee at Government House, Halifax, Nova Scotia. (The *Illustrated London News* Picture Library)

contemporary accounts people had talked, thought and dreamed of nothing but the Prince of Wales and how he should be received. His name was to be seen everywhere, even appearing mysteriously in advertisements for Halifax's national dish of pork and beans, and it was jocularly said that one could not sit down to a meal without Edward's portrait appearing through the gravy on one's dinner plate. This intense interest encompassed the Prince's wardrobe – what would he wear? In fact he made his public appearances either in his smart uniform as Colonel in the Guards, or else wearing conventional morning dress consisting of a long, dark, neatly fitting frock-coat, light-coloured trousers, smart waistcoat, bow tie or stock, walking cane or umbrella, gloves and a light-coloured or white top hat. All these items were eagerly observed and quickly copied. By this stage of the tour the royal visitor, as his entourage noted, had entered completely into the 'spirit of the thing'. At the Halifax Celebration Ball Edward, like his mother a most accomplished dancer, delighted his hosts and the guests by dancing until a quarter to four in the morning. None the less he was up early to hold a levee – a ceremonial morning reception – for the town dignitaries.

Brief calls at Fredericton, New Brunswick and Charlottetown on Prince Edward Island followed, and by 11 August *Hero* had reached Gaspe Bay at the mouth of the St Lawrence river. Here Sir Edmund Head, Governor-General of the Canadas, and members of his Cabinet came on board. On 18 August *Hero* anchored off Quebec and Edward landed to continue his journey across the continent by river steamer and train. Quebec, splendidly decorated with flags and arches, played host to the Prince for five days. Residing in the old Parliament House, specially fitted up for the occasion, he was given a 100-strong guard of honour as his escort for various functions. These included levees, receptions, processions, conferring knighthoods on the Speakers of the two Legislative Chambers, and visiting the city's monuments as well as viewing the famous battlefields on the Heights of Abraham where the British

Edward's arrival in Quebec.
(The *Illustrated London News* Picture Library)

Edward in Montreal, laying the last stone of the Victoria Bridge.
(The *Illustrated London News* Picture Library)

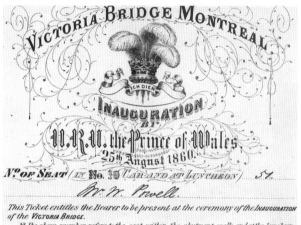

Invitation card for the inauguration of the Victoria Bridge by the Prince, and for the luncheon, on 25 August 1860.
(National Archives of Canada)

General James Wolfe died in 1759. A much appreciated entertainment was the ball given by the Mayor of Quebec. At this glittering event Edward gratified all those present, displaying his evident enjoyment, and the exuberance of youth, by dancing every one of the twenty-two dances on the programme.

From Quebec the royal party, escorted by a large fleet of lake and up-river steamers, proceeded by river steamer up the St Lawrence river to Montreal. Here the Prince performed the ceremony which was one of the specific purposes of his tour, the inauguration of the Victoria Bridge across the St Lawrence river. An open railway car had been specially built and beautifully decorated to transport the royal visitor and his hosts across this imposing engineering construction almost 2 miles in length. Crowds of spectators greeted the Prince's arrival. He performed the ceremony of laying the last stone, a huge 10-ton slab which was lowered into place. Edward then got on the car and was driven to the centre of the bridge to clinch the last rivet, where all was in readiness with two workmen waiting with their big hammers.

When he was handed the heavy hammer he swung it up stoutly, but held it with the big, or wrong, end foremost – only a professional smith would have known which end to use. When this mistake was pointed out to him, he laughed, reversed the hammer and gave the last rivet, a silver one, some resounding blows. The party then travelled on the car right across the bridge to the far side of the river and back again for a grand luncheon party.

The programme in Montreal was crammed with events; the Prince opened an Industrial Exhibition, heard the famous prima donna Adelina Patti sing at a concert (he was to meet her again in America), and attended a splendid ball. For this festive occasion a huge tent, 100 yards in diameter, had been erected to form a circular ballroom. Inside all round the edge and about 12 feet above ground level a gallery of seats had been built. Under the gallery a raised dais and a retiring room had been arranged for the visitor and his party. The tent, all pink, white and gold, was garlanded with flowers and greenery, the ceiling was painted and the whole illuminated with gas burners to give a delightful effect. Edward arrived at ten o'clock and started the dancing. The first

Edward in Ottawa, laying the corner-stone for the parliament buildings. (The *Illustrated London News* Picture Library)

The Lumber Arch in Union Square, Ottawa, constructed for Edward's visit. (National Archives of Canada)

Edward in Ottawa, going down the timber-slide.
(The *Illustrated London News* Picture Library)

quadrille was danced to the tune which had almost become the Prince's signature tune throughout Canada, 'Jamais je ne t'oublierai' ('I shall never forget you'), being played for him at his every arrival and departure. To the delight of his hosts and the whole assembly he danced with evident enjoyment all through the night until the ball ended at five o'clock in the morning.

The royal party travelled from Montreal on to Ottawa where on 1 September in a gaily decorated pavilion, the heir performed the second official ceremony of his tour by laying the cornerstone of the Parliament House planned for the two provinces of the united colony. But, this completed, the lumber town of Ottawa – one of the triumphal arches in Union Square was ingeniously constructed entirely of logs – offered the young royal visitor a unique experience much more to his liking. This was a ride on a raft or 'crib' of logs down a timber-slide in the river. Watched by thousands of excited spectators, the Prince and his party walked along a boom to where the crib, about 25 feet wide and made up of logs lashed together, was moored. The timber-slide was an inclined plane with a depth of a few feet of water rushing over it to form a waterway over which the crib could pass without mishap, the purpose being to get the logs over stony places in the river where they might otherwise be damaged. When the crib was launched it slid away down the plane with great speed; water flew up over the front and the men riding the raft had to stand firm to withstand the speed and vibrations, and be alert for the accidents which sometimes happened. As the be-flagged royal raft shot past down the slide, the spectators cramming the banks and all the available bridges cheered and applauded wildly. To the relief of all, the raft passed down safely with, on board, a delighted Prince whose only regret was that the 'shoot' was not at least a mile longer.

The welcome ceremony for Edward in Toronto.
(The *Illustrated London News* Picture Library)

From Ottawa the royal party proceeded to Brockville, brilliantly lit up to welcome the visitor, and passed on to Kingston. But here sectarian rivalry threatened to disrupt the trip. Although Edward had scrupulously observed complete impartiality between the claims on his participation put forward by the French Catholics and the Protestant Orangemen, the Orange majority of the inhabitants of Kingston were determined to greet the royal visitor solely as the descendant of their hero and patron saint, King William III. Arches and banners were lavishly decorated with pictures of 'King Billy' and the town was ablaze with orange flags and badges. The Duke of Newcastle, seeing all this preparation, promptly decided that the Prince of Wales must not lend himself, however innocently, to what could only be considered as a sectarian demonstration and ordered the steamer carrying the party to sail on without stopping at the landing stage. Bitter arguments ensued among the disappointed townspeople of Kingston, with the result that a deputation was sent on to the next stopping place, Toronto, to try to make their peace with the royal visitor. In Toronto itself Orangemen arches were already in place along the route which Edward would take to Government House, where he was to stay for a week. Requested by the Duke of Newcastle to remove these arches, the Mayor complied, but unfortunately one arch, displaying a picture of 'King Billy' at the Battle of the Boyne, was overlooked and remained in place during the royal procession. The Duke of Newcastle sternly rebuked the Mayor and cancelled his invitation to the royal levee, whereupon the furious and disappointed Mayor refused to apologise. This disagreeable situation was soon resolved, however. The deputation from Kingston arrived and was forgiven and the Mayor of Toronto was invited to another levee where the young Prince consoled and charmed this tearful guest with assurances that his loyalty and sincerity were thoroughly appreciated by himself and the Queen.

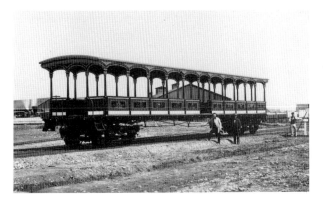

Edward contributed to the prestige of Canadian Railways by formally inaugurating the Victoria Tubular Bridge, and by travelling during his trip on a special train. This photograph shows the Observation Car, which was built for him in Canada by Canadian craftsmen.
(National Archives of Canada)

Royal ❦ Train!

GRAND TRUNK RAILWAY.

TORONTO TO LONDON.

Wednesday, 12th September, 1860.

Inter. Dist.	Total Dist.	STATIONS.	TORONTO TIME.		Inter. Dist.	Total Dist.	STATIONS.	TORONTO TIME.
Leave		Toronto	11.00 A.M.	Leave	7	57	SHANTZ	1.35 P.
1	1	GRAND JUNCTION	11.66 "		2	59	BRESLAU	1.40 "
4¼	5¼	CARLTON	11.15 "		5	64	Berlin	1.52 "
3¾	9	WESTON	11.22 "		6	70	PETERSBURG	2.04 "
7	16	MALTON	11.37 "		3	73	BADEN	2.12 "
6	22	BRAMPTON	11.50 "		3	76	HAMBURGH	2.18 "
5	27	NORVAL	12.00 M.		7	83	SHAKSPEARE	2.32 Crn.
3	30	Georgetown	12.10 P.M.		6	89	Stratford	2.44 A. 2.54 D.
2¼	32¼	LIME HOUSE	12.18 "		10	99	St. Mary's	3.15 P.
3½	36	ACTON WEST	12.28 "		11	110	THORNDALE	3.38 "
6	42	ROCKWOOD	12.42 "		10	120	London	4.00 A.
8	50	Guelph	1.00 A. 1.20 D.					

Special Rules for Wednesday, the 12th September, 1860.

No. 1—NUMBERS 7, 8, 9 AND 10 TRAINS will not run.
No. 2—No IRREGULAR TRAIN or ENGINE will be allowed on main line.
No. 3—NUMBER ONE EXPRESS will wait at Shakspeare, the arrival of the Royal Train.
No. 4—NUMBER TWO EXPRESS will leave Toronto at 11.30 a. m., and keep HALF AN HOUR behind the Royal Train at every Station.
No. 5—A PILOT ENGINE will run exactly 10 MINUTES AHEAD of the Royal Train.
No. 6—STATION AGENTS AND THEIR ASSISTANTS must be on duty and assist in keeping back any crowd of people at Stations.
No. 7—CARE MUST BE TAKEN to ENSURE SAFETY by every employee, and Signal Flags must be shown at each Station.
WHITE, if Track is clear.
GREEN, if Pilot Engine is less than 10 minutes ahead of Royal Train.
RED, if Track is obstructed.

Timetable for the Royal Train from Toronto to London, a journey which would take two days on horseback, but which Edward made by train in five hours.
(By kind permission of the Canadian High Commission)

From Toronto Edward travelled across Canada on the Grand Trunk Railway in a carriage specially built for him. On 12 September he arrived in London to find the town crowded with thousands of visitors waiting to give him an enthusiastic welcome and escort him to the Tecumseh Hotel. In the evening he watched a procession of some 1,500 torch-bearers; in Stratford a thousand schoolchildren greeted him with a rendering of the National Anthem, and in Guelph he was serenaded by twenty-nine young ladies and delighted his audience by kissing the daughter of the Mayor by way of thanks for this charming entertainment. From Sarnia, the farthest point reached by the

Edward and his suite at Point View, Niagara. (National Archives of Canada)

The acrobat Blondin carrying a man across his high wire over Niagara Falls. Edward watched him perform a similar feat. (Kiwanis Collection, Niagara Falls Public Library)

railway, the party retraced their steps to pay a visit to the Niagara Falls. For this visit, ostensibly a personal one without pomp or state, Edward had been lent a house, while his suite were lodged in cottages in the garden of the Clifton Hotel. But the private nature of his visit did not prevent huge crowds from assembling, nor did it deter a project to illuminate the Falls in his honour, something never before attempted. Two hundred huge Bengal Lights had been manufactured. Distributed around the Falls, under the cliffs and behind the great falling sheet of water itself, they were all lit simultaneously at ten o'clock in the evening, exploding into sparkling brilliancy so that the waters, according to the dazzled onlookers, resembled sheets of crystal and cascades of diamonds. The day after this triumphant display, the Prince witnessed a performance which had thrilled audiences at the Falls since the previous year, when Blondin, a young French acrobat, had first traversed the Falls on a tightrope slung across the chasm. Blondin's stunts on his high wire, high above the boiling gorge, included carrying a man across on his back, wheeling a man in a barrow, stopping in mid-rope to pull up a bottle of water from the Falls, cooking and eating an omelette, sitting and lying on the rope, turning somersaults and other hair-raising tricks. For the benefit of the royal visitor and the thousands of breathless spectators, Blondin took a man over the rope, returning on stilts – a feat he had never before attempted. The acrobat's offer to take the Prince over with him was sportingly accepted by the young man, but rejected with horror by his aghast suite, and Edward later viewed the Falls, not from Blondin's tightrope, but from the deck of the little steamer *Maid of the Mist* and from the slippery path behind the curtain of falling water.

The Prince's visit to Canada was almost over; his last public engagements were in Hamilton where on 18 September he addressed thousands of farmers at the annual Provincial Exhibition of Upper Canada. And then at the little frontier town of Windsor, he bade farewell to the Governor-General and members of the Canadian Government, at the end of what was recognised by all as an outstandingly successful trip. The heir had undergone a rigorous schedule of engagements; he had replied to dozens of addresses, shaken thousands of hands, appeared in countless processions, attended lunches, dinners, levees and balls and throughout it all, as his Governor and members of his suite had to admit, had maintained an appearance of interest, good humour, pleasure and even delight. Nobly representing the Queen, he had charmed his audiences to an unexpected degree. An amazing change had taken place in the son considered so 'unsatisfactory' by Victoria and Albert. Would the tour through republican America be an anti-climax?

The answer became clear as soon as the royal visitor set foot on American soil. From his first appearance in Detroit on 20 September until his ships left Portland on 20 October, the Prince's 'private visit' became another triumphal progress. The enthusiastic reception, the huge crowds who gathered wherever Edward appeared, the scramble for tickets at every function he attended, may initially have been due to the natural curiosity of a young democracy about an ancient royal line in general, but as the tour progressed, it became obvious that it was largely the manners and demeanour of the Prince himself, with his easy, genial, frank and yet dignified bearing, which accounted for the welcome. Travelling on special trains in a director's car, and with crowds thronging every station whether his train stopped or not, Edward proceeded westwards to Chicago, where he was shown the big grain elevators and the unusual sight of a wooden dwelling-house being moved to a new site on huge wooden rollers. His American hosts then offered their guest a weekend of his most preferred sport, shooting. The party stayed in the little prairie village of Dwight. Immediately on arrival the young heir was out with his gun, proving himself the best shot with a good bag of prairie chicken and quail, some of which he selected to be stuffed and sent home. After this pleasant interlude, on went the party to St Louis; the annual Fair was in full swing and the town crowded with tens of thousands of visitors. Edward thoroughly enjoyed the Fair; he inspected the cattle and produce, watched the trotting-races for over three hours and finally bought himself a fine fast-trotting horse (horses were one of his lifelong interests). On 28 September the party set off on the long train ride to Cincinnati, where they put up at the huge Burnet House Hotel. Crowds were waiting outside the hotel to catch a glimpse of the young visitor and answer the questions all the ladies had been asking: 'How did he look? How was he dressed? Was he pretty? What was the colour of his hair?' The

The Burnet House Hotel in Cincinnati where Edward and his suite occupied twenty-nine rooms. This huge luxury hotel had an elegant drawing-room, which could accommodate six to eight hundred people, and a reading-room supplied with two or three hundred weekly and daily newspapers.
(The *Illustrated London News* Picture Library)

Pike's Opera House in Cincinnati, where a reception ball was held for the Prince on Saturday 29 September 1860.
(Collection of the Public Library of Cincinnati and Hamilton County)

Prince drove round the town, paid visits, attended church, listened with 'much kindness and consideration' to an old soldier who had served for twelve years in the British Army, threw a bouquet to two lucky young ladies and danced until midnight at a grand ball held in the opera house.

On rushed the royal train to Pittsburgh, where another enthusiastic reception was waiting. The plan was to drive the visitor round the town, but, unfortunately, the Mayor had ordered the militia and bands preceding the royal carriage to keep to a slow march. The result was that the population of Pittsburgh walked alongside the carriage, peering closely into the Prince's face and chatting with him, for an hour and a half. Edward manfully endured this flattering, though trying, manifestation of interest and friendliness with a modest and good-humoured courtesy which won all hearts. As his train steamed out of the station, the band again played his 'signature-tune', the charming Canadian air 'I shall never forget you.' A historic moment came at the next stop, Harrisburg, when, at the Governor's request, the Prince sat in the chair in which the Declaration of Independence had been signed. At Baltimore he was shown Washington's monument, and on 3 October he arrived at the White House for a three-day stay with President Buchanan. Edward liked the fatherly President and admired his pretty niece who acted as hostess. The crowded programme included sightseeing tours, dinners, receptions and a firework display. On 5 October Edward visited the former house of George Washington and, in a simple yet solemn ceremony, planted a chestnut tree on his grave. President Buchanan and his young guest parted with regret, and each wrote warmly to Victoria about the visit.

A brief stay in Richmond, Virginia, arranged to give the visitor a glimpse of the slave-owning South, was followed by two days in Philadelphia, which the Prince considered the prettiest town he had seen in America. Electioneering for a new Governor, with the controversy over slavery as its main issue, was in full swing as the royal party arrived on 10 October, and Edward enjoyed a lively night, strolling round the town to see the bonfires and torchlight processions. Electioneering fever, the return of a Republican anti-slavery candidate, and the general satisfaction that their royal visitor had witnessed at first hand the workings of democracy, did not prevent vast crowds from flocking to see the Prince of Wales or prevent the whole audience from rising as he entered the opera house in the evening and remaining standing throughout the playing of 'God Save the Queen' – an unheard-of occurrence. The opera performed was Von Flotow's *Martha* (perhaps selected as a delicate

The coloratura soprano Adelina Patti (1843–1919), who sang for Edward at a Montreal concert, seen here in the title role of Von Flotow's opera *Martha*, which she performed for the Prince in Philadelphia. (National Portrait Gallery, London; photograph by Camille Silvy, *c*.1861)

compliment to the royal visitor, since the action takes place in Richmond Park and the main character is a lady-in-waiting to Queen Anne). Adelina Patti, who had already sung for the Prince in Montreal, sang the leading role. Edward, for whom opera was to remain a lasting passion throughout his life and who was to hear Patti many times again, wrote admiringly to his mother of her 'very pretty voice'. Another encounter in Philadelphia was of quite a different nature. The visitor was taken to see the huge, modernised State Penitentiary, where he was introduced to one of the inmates, a judge condemned for forgery. When he rather tentatively enquired if this unfortunate prisoner would like to speak with him, the judge responded cheerfully: 'Talk away, Prince! I'm here for twenty years and have plenty of time!' A quick glimpse of a race-track to see horses running on sand and gravel instead of turf concluded the visit, and the party sped on to New York to be overwhelmed by one of the most tumultuous welcomes of the trip.

Landing by boat at the Emigrants' Wharf, Edward was immediately plunged into public appearances. Rushed into a nearby house to change into his Guards' uniform, he was then called upon to inspect 6,000 militiamen drawn up on parade on the Wharf. The troops then formed themselves into ranks to precede the Prince's carriage at a walking pace to the City Hall, where they executed a smart march-past. All this took place before a deliriously excited crowd some 300,000 strong, whose number and enthusiasm astonished both Edward – who wrote to his mother: 'I never dreamed we would be received as we were' – and his suite. Even General Bruce, never prone to exaggeration, admitted that New York's reception had outdone all its predecessors. Darkness fell before the slow-moving procession reached the Fifth Avenue Hotel, a resplendent building of white marble, where the Prince waved to the crowd from his balcony and told his delighted hosts that his rooms were far more comfortable than any he had at home. Of the entertainments offered to the visitor, the high point was the Grand Ball at the Academy of Music. Tickets

The ball given in Edward's honour in New York at the Academy of Music.
(The *Illustrated London News* Picture Library)

had been limited to 3,000, but another 2,000 would-be guests rushed through the barriers into the beautifully decorated ballroom. Edward and his party arrived at half-past ten, to be hemmed in by eager onlookers. At this exciting moment, under the weight of a jostling 5,000-strong assembly, part of the wooden floor gave way, sinking slowly about 3 feet. Fortunately no one was hurt; carpenters were rushed in to repair the damage, which they accomplished so quickly that one of their number was nailed down under the floorboards and had to knock furiously to be released. Dancing began at midnight, the floor held firm and in spite of the crush Edward danced happily until dawn. A great procession with some 6,000 torch-bearers and a visit through enormous crowds to Trinity Church – where, for the first time since 1776, prayers were said for the Royal Family – rounded off this outstanding triumph of the young Prince, aptly summed up by one popular American writer who declared: 'He may consider himself a lucky lad if he escape a nomination for President before he reaches his homeward-bound Fleet!'

On 14 October the party was off on its last lap to Boston and another great welcome. Putting up at the Revere Hotel, Edward rode out to inspect a parade of militia on the Common. One of the spectators was Longfellow; the poet described the splendid day – 'a perfect illumination of sunshine and golden leaves' – and how the Prince looked 'remarkably well on horseback'. Longfellow was presented to the young heir, and went with his party to the Grand Ball in the opera house that evening. (This was not to be the only contact between poet and Prince; Edward, who already possessed an attractive quality unusual in a young person, that of 'keeping up with' and not 'dropping' acquaintances, was some years later instrumental in getting a monument to Longfellow placed in Westminster Abbey.) Two other well-known American writers, Ralph Waldo Emerson and Oliver Wendell Holmes, were also presented to the Prince. Visits to Bunker's Hill, Harvard University, Boston's large public library and a music festival rounded off the programme.

(Above) Henry Wadsworth Longfellow
(1807–1882), photographed by G W Bacon
& Co in 1882.
(National Portrait Gallery, London)

(Above right) Oliver Wendell Holmes
(1809–1894).
(National Portrait Gallery, London)

(Right) Ralph Waldo Emerson (1803–1882).
(National Portrait Gallery, London;
photograph by J W Black of Boston, USA)

At Portland *Hero* was waiting to take Edward home. Members of the Canadian Government and American representatives assembled on board. The Prince, in fine form, gently teased the Governor of Maine, whose State prohibited the consumption of alcohol, by asking if he would take a little wine, or did the Maine law apply on board ship? To which sally the Governor jovially responded that he was out of his jurisdiction and would take the consequences. In this happy mood farewells were said and *Hero* sailed out of

HMS *Hero*, with escort ships, setting off home from Portland, USA.
(The *Illustrated London News* Picture Library)

Portland Harbour on 20 October for a return journey, hampered by fog, huge seas and gales, of twenty-six days.

The heir to the throne arrived home to general congratulations. His father and mother, at first amazed by the glowing reports in every mail, were generous in their approval, Albert declaring somewhat wryly that his son was now 'generally pronounced to be the most perfect production of nature', Victoria observing to her eldest daughter, married to the Crown Prince of Prussia, that 'he was immensely popular everywhere and really deserves the highest praise', adding rather guiltily, 'all the more as he was never spared any reproof'. The general public, who had followed the tour in the illustrated newspapers, was proud of the exploits of their Prince, while the politicians, with very few exceptions, welcomed the strengthening of ties between the countries. And what of the effect on Edward himself of his marvellous voyage to the New World? It was obvious to most observers that with his qualities of patience, good humour, tact, good manners, dignity, ability to say a kind word when required and, especially, his ability to listen – qualities not often found in young persons – together with his powers of observation and memory, Edward was absolutely cut out to become a most successful public figure. The Prince of Wales had in fact found his *métier* and a new world of his own.

3

A MARRIAGE HAS BEEN ARRANGED

*P*RINCE EDWARD may have realised that he had accomplished his emancipation; his parents, unfortunately, did not. Within a few days of his triumphal return home, the young man was packed off again to Oxford, Albert bemoaning the fact that the slow homeward voyage had deprived his son of almost half a term's tuition. Edward renewed his pleas to be allowed to undergo the military training on which he had set his heart, an inclination which had been much stimulated by all his military engagements on his trip. But General Bruce harped on the 'temptations' of military life, Albert was adamant, and back to Frewin Hall with his usual suite, including the Governor, went the reluctant scholar, finding life sadly flat. At Christmas the Prince bade farewell to Oxford, only to be enrolled immediately, following Albert's plan, at the University of Cambridge in January 1861. Again, he was not allowed to enjoy the social side of undergraduate life by living in college and mixing with his contemporaries. Instead, a country mansion, Madingley Hall, some 4 miles out of town, was rented to accommodate the Prince, General and Mrs Bruce and the rest of the entourage. While Albert, inspecting the house, complained that not enough space had been provided for the young student's books, his son was far more interested in the 'capital' stables and the possibility of hunting – a sport deplored by his mother who begged him not to break his neck.

Edward, however, was to find his studies more palatable to him than might at first have been expected. Among his tutors he found a congenial teacher. Charles Kingsley, author of historical romances and social reformer (who later wrote the famous *Water Babies*), occupied at that time the Chair of Modern History at Cambridge and had been selected by Albert to teach his son history. Kingsley, at first, on his own confession, nervous, worried about the responsibility of his task and agitated by receiving strict and detailed instructions from

Charles Kingsley (1819–1875), who taught Edward at Cambridge. A pen-and-ink sketch by William S Hunt, after a photograph of 1874.
(National Portrait Gallery, London)

Albert on how he was to conduct his lectures and what he was to teach, was pleasantly surprised by his pupil. He found the Prince 'jolly' and interesting, asking very intelligent questions and listening attentively to the answers. Kingsley taught Edward in his house twice a week with a small select group of undergraduates, and every Saturday the young man rode over to see his tutor alone and go over the week's work with him. Soon teacher and pupil were on the most cordial terms, and a firm friendship developed which lasted until the Professor's premature death in 1875. With his new-found self-confidence and charm, the Prince in fact was managing to make friends and live his own life to some extent, while outwardly still conforming cheerfully to his father's strict discipline.

All this had at last the desired result, when Albert and the Governor agreed that a spell of military training during the summer vacation at the Curragh camp near Dublin might not be such a bad thing after all. Edward's joy was somewhat quenched, however, when he realised that this was to be as much of a 'cramming' exercise as his 'book-learning' had been. Albert drew up a detailed memorandum, which had to be signed by the military chiefs, requiring his son to pass all the grades of instruction from ensign to commanding a brigade in ten weeks – a schedule to daunt even the most enthusiastic professional soldier. As for the convivial dinners he had been looking forward to in the officers' mess, he found that his off-duty time was to be strictly regulated, with evenings devoted to serious reading and writing. None the less, the Prince contrived to amuse himself at the Curragh, and even found time to indulge in an amorous pursuit, when his fellow officers smuggled a pretty and lively young actress, Nellie Clifden, known to them all, into his quarters – a light-hearted, youthful escapade which was to have unhappy consequences.

The thoughts of the young heir's parents had also been turning towards the tender passions, or rather to the institution of marriage. They had earnestly agreed, for some time past, that the best method of 'saving' their son and 'keeping him straight' would be for him to contract an early marriage. But where to find the paragon of a princess who would fulfil their stringent requirements of a good disposition, satisfactory health, education, character and looks? Albert drew up a short-list of seven prospective brides and photographs were shown to the Prince – understandably very lukewarm about the whole affair and declaring manfully that he intended to marry only for love. Six of the girls were rejected by Victoria and Albert for various reasons: they were too young, delicate, practising Roman Catholics, had unpleasant parents and so on. The remaining candidate was a schoolgirl of sixteen, modest, unaffected and natural, and outstandingly beautiful. She was the daughter of Prince Christian of Denmark, heir to the throne of that country, and her name was Alexandra. This charming girl had not been seriously considered initially as a prospective bride, for reasons both personal and political. On the personal side Victoria and Albert disliked the Hesse-Cassel family, to which Alexandra's mother belonged. The political position was more complicated: by family relationships and inclination Victoria and Albert were pro-German, and the recent marriage of their eldest daughter to the Crown Prince of Prussia had served to strengthen these ties. Prussia had for long coveted the two Duchies of Schleswig and Holstein over which the King of Denmark ruled. Legal and political arguments were raging over the fate of these Duchies, and it was becoming obvious to all onlookers that growing German nationalism would eventually force the issue, possibly choosing the

Speyer Cathedral, scene of the first meeting between Edward and Alexandra. Engraving by Joseph Maximilian Koch from a drawing by Ludwig Rohbock, c.1850, printed and published by G G Lange in Darmstadt.
(Historisches Museum der Pfalz, Speyer)

moment when Alexandra's father became King – as indeed was to prove the case. The Prince's parents therefore felt at first that to promote the match would be to give the impression that England was siding with Denmark. But a number of factors contrived to make them change their minds: their anxiety to get their son married, the dearth of suitable candidates, the rumours that other partners were being proposed for Alexandra, and their eldest daughter's own warm espousal – against German feelings – of the Danish princess, brought matters to a head. At the end of his time at the Curragh camp Edward, displaying no enthusiasm, was despatched to Germany, ostensibly to view military manoeuvres with his brother-in-law, the Crown Prince, but in reality to see Alexandra 'by accident'.

The place chosen by the Crown Princess for the meeting of the two young people was the Cathedral at Speyer. On 24 September two groups of 'tourists' made their way to this famous monument, Alexandra with her father and mother, and the Prince with his Governor, his sister and brother-in-law. Although Edward was travelling incognito, the bishop immediately recognised him and eagerly began to show him the cathedral treasures. The Crown Princess hastily intervened, begging the bishop to show her the beautiful frescoes, and Edward and Alexandra were left alone for a few moments before the Altar of St Bernard to make each other's acquaintance. The whole party then had lunch and returned to Heidelberg, where on the following day, after an exchange of photographs, the young people said farewell. Letters were soon winging their way from Heidelberg to the anxious parents at home: an elated report from the Crown Princess, enthusing over Alexandra's sweetness of expression, grace of manner, refinement, loveliness and general suitability – although having to admit that her brother had found Alexandra's nose too

37

long and her forehead too low – and a more restrained and diplomatic missive from the Prince, declaring that 'the young lady of whom I have heard so much' was charming and very pretty, but that he would wait until he got home before discussing the matter fully. This drew predictable reactions from the parents. The Queen, who, although usually intelligent and perceptive in her summing-up of people, displayed an almost complete lack of understanding of her son's character and temperament, burst out angrily to her daughter that although Edward 'meant well' she thought he was incapable of love or of any other enthusiasm – a strange misreading. Albert, in a meticulous and coolly worded memorandum, pointed out to his son all the difficulties, political and otherwise, which could arise if he refused to commit himself.

On 13 October Edward returned to Cambridge to complete his studies, leaving affairs in this rather unsatisfactory state. But much worse was to follow. Gossip about his amorous escapade at the Curragh camp, which had been circulating in London for some time, had reached the Court by November and finally came to the ears of Albert who, unwisely, carried it to Victoria. The horror, revulsion and anguish of the parents was overpowering. Despairing reproaches and angry admonitions fell on the head of the hapless Prince, who was exhorted to confess everything to his Governor. On 25 November, although Albert was very unwell, he found time to rush to Madingley Hall to 'have it out' with his son. He found Edward suitably contrite, although adamant in refusing to name his brother-officers who had instigated the affair – an attitude Albert appreciated. Father and son became reconciled during a long walk, and Albert returned to Windsor, happier in mind but physically exhausted. He was in fact already suffering from typhoid, although the disease was not diagnosed until it was too late. Albert died on 14 December in the evening. The distraught Queen who, in her anguish, threw all the blame for Albert's illness on her son, had refused to summon him to the dying man's bedside. In the end it was his sister Alice who sent him a telegram, but one so enigmatically worded that Edward, who had been taking his examinations at Cambridge and had no idea of the gravity of the situation, first fulfilled a dinner engagement and arrived at the Castle at three o'clock on the morning of the 14th in cheerful mood. He was aghast to find his father on his death-bed, delirious and unable to recognise him. In the evening, still in a state of shock, he knelt at the foot of his father's bed and witnessed his last moments; afterwards he threw himself impulsively into the arms of his prostrate mother, vowing to be all he could to her, and she embraced him lovingly. Albert's funeral took place on 23 December at St George's Chapel, Windsor. The Prince was the Chief Mourner for the man he always described as the best and kindest of fathers. Onlookers described slight, fair-haired young Edward's comportment upon this occasion – very erect, walking firmly and resolutely with an air of dignified resignation. On the afternoon of the funeral he joined the Queen at Osborne House on the Isle of Wight, to which she had retreated.

The emotional reconciliation between mother and son was short-lived. Victoria was soon writing to her daughter and confidante, the Crown Princess of Prussia, that she still held the Prince responsible for Albert's death, that she could not see him without a shudder and that she could not bear to have him about the house. This uncomfortable situation was immediately noticed by politicians and public; there was talk of a serious estrangement between the monarch and her heir, and the Prime Minister, Lord Palmerston, felt impelled to intervene. The Queen, put on the defensive, protested that Edward was a

Edward walking in the funeral procession of his father, Prince Albert. Beside him, dressed in Highland costume, is his little brother Arthur, observed by onlookers to be crying bitterly. (The *Illustrated London News* Picture Library)

good and dutiful son but that, nevertheless, it would be best for him to go away for a while. Albert had decided to complete his son's studies with an educational tour of the Middle East, and all his carefully made plans were ready at the time of his death. On this tour, therefore, the Prince must go. On 5 February 1862 Victoria and her 'Poor Boy', as she called him, both in tears, said farewell and the heir left England again.

Arthur Penrhyn Stanley (1815–1881), Dean of Westminster, Edward's tutor and companion on his tour of the Middle East in 1862. Chalk drawing by Emily J Harding. (National Portrait Gallery, London)

The young Prince, upset by his mother's behaviour, debarred from any entertainment during the period of strict mourning and in any case travelling incognito, set off in a mood of deep gloom and despondency. Nor was his Governor, who was as usual in charge of the party, in happier mood. He had received minute instructions from the Queen to prepare Edward for the likelihood of her early death (one of her recurrent nervous fears), to keep him engaged in 'useful pursuits' and above all to foster assiduously Albert's last plan, that of the proposed Danish marriage. But as the subdued party progressed through Vienna, where they were entertained by Franz Joseph, Emperor of Austria, and Venice, by his Empress Elizabeth, visited Corfu and paused in Albania to shoot wild boar, spirits were rising.

The Royal Yacht *Osborne* reached Egypt on 28 February. Here another, initially gloomy, member joined the party. Dr Arthur Stanley, the Oxford Professor of Ecclesiastical History and one of the Prince's former teachers, had, rather against his will, been persuaded by the Queen to guide her son round the antiquities and archaeological treasures, and privately anticipated a tedious and frustrating time for himself. However, he soon changed his mind. On 2 March, although slightly deploring a jolly ride by the Prince through the streets of Cairo on a white donkey called 'Captain Snook', he noticed with surprise immediately afterwards a little incident which illustrated Edward's quickness of memory and courtesy. In the English church Edward recognised a man with whom he had once played tennis at Oxford and whom he had not known would be in Cairo; he requested Stanley to bring this man over and chatted to him for some time. On 6 March the Prince started at dawn and enjoyed an energetic scramble up the Great Pyramid, a popular excursion. Stanley was anxious about his safety on the smooth, slippery stones and insisted on sending a little Bedouin boy up beside him lest he tumbled, but Edward accomplished his climb without difficulty. The party then embarked on two steamers and set off up the Nile, the Prince with his gun at the ready, as there was plenty of rough shooting to be had. By this time Stanley was being gradually won over by the Prince's charm. He wrote home: 'It is impossible not to like him', and was gratified by his charge's agreement that there should be no shooting on Sundays (unless a crocodile appeared) and by his 'most reasonable and proper remarks on the due observance of Sunday in England'.

Edward visited the Great Pyramid and the Great Sphinx at Giza on his Middle East tour in 1862. This photograph was taken in 1858 by Francis Frith, an early travel photographer. (Scottish National Portrait Gallery, Edinburgh)

Expeditions were made from the ships to visit temples and monuments on the way. Edward, who would rather have been shooting or practising physical sports, submitted gracefully to being instructed about antiquities. Stanley was also discovering how to interest his pupil. On 15 March at the Temple of Edfu where excavations had been carried out, they found the place where the Sacred Hawk had been kept. Stanley wrote: 'I went over it all first with His Royal Highness who expressed considerable interest. He entered with keen delight into my wish that he should shoot and carry off a hawk which was flying over the Temple.' On 18 March, after leaving Thebes, they watched together as a tomb was excavated at their request, revealing a mummy which they suspected had been placed there especially for them. By now Stanley was writing about the Prince's 'astonishing memory of persons and places' and admitting: 'There is more to him that I thought.' After going as far as the First Cataract, back steamed the ships to Cairo, where Stanley was greeted by the sad news that his mother had died. Edward's tactful and sincere sympathy touched the bereaved man, who decided to carry on with the tour.

Osborne reached Jaffa on 31 March and the party disembarked, to continue their journey travelling on horseback, living in tents and studying Biblical sites under Stanley's guidance. On 'perfectly easy and friendly' terms, Prince and Professor stood together on the hill from which England's King Richard I and his Crusaders had first seen Jerusalem. 'The Prince was dressed,' wrote Stanley, 'as he now usually is in travelling, in a long white robe thrown over his coat, to keep off the heat and dust. It becomes him remarkably well and gives a dignity and grace to his whole appearance.' A motley procession formed up behind the Prince to ride into the city. The rest of his suite, a long

41

line of mounted spearsmen who were guarding the party, some English clergymen, Franciscan monks, Greek clergy and swarms of children singing hymns all stumbled along the stony uneven road. To Stanley it was 'all like a dream'. As he rode beside the Prince, he pointed out and explained to him all the Biblical references, a flock of white sheep and black goats, fortuitously grazing on a nearby hillside, served as 'the framework of the great Parable delivered also from this hillside on the "Day of Judgement"'. At Hebron Edward 'pulled rank' for the first time in a determined, and successful effort to get the authorities to open, for Stanley's inspection, the Tomb of Abraham, situated under the Great Mosque and jealously guarded. 'I went to the Prince,' wrote the delighted Stanley, 'to thank him, and to express how, but for him, I should never had had this great opportunity. "Well," he said with touching, almost reproachful simplicity, "high station, you see, has after all some merits, some advantages".'

On went the cavalcade to Nazareth which they reached on Good Friday. A decision to ride up Mount Carmel to view the sunset did not please Edward, who wanted to go quail-shooting, but he gave in with good grace, as Stanley observed with pleasure: 'So he came, and though the ride up and down the mountain was very hard, he expressed no ill-humour, and listened at the top, with the best grace possible, to my explanation of the view, and discussed with real good sense and feeling the slaughter of the prophets of Baal and Mendelssohn's *Elijah*.' After an Easter Day service in the tents pitched on the lake shore by the old walls of Tiberias, the party moved on to Damascus. 'You must imagine us,' wrote Stanley, 'winding down some hillside. In front is usually H.R.H. in his white robe, with his gun by his side. Scampering over everybody in violent haste to be close to H.R.H. comes the long army of fifty mounted spearsmen, their red pennons flashing through the rocks and thickets as they mount and descend.' Stanley had even become reconciled to the young Prince's passion for shooting – 'As for the shooting, it is satisfactory to reflect that he is so heartily devoted to such an innocent, healthy and absorbing occupation' – and was taking an interest in the animals being collected as they travelled about: 'the Prince has got two little wild boars and two little leopards, that are being brought up by a cat that we took from Alexandria. The leopards are so small that it is difficult to know whether they are really leopards or only wild kittens. But they sleep in the Prince's tent, and we shall soon know.' After Damascus, Beirut, a glimpse of the sea ports of Tyre and Sidon, and the Cedars of Lebanon from the deck of the *Osborne*, and the tour was nearly over. Shedding his incognito, Edward attended a State Breakfast with the Sultan at Constantinople, had brief stopovers in Athens and Malta and made his way home through France.

From Stanley's reflections on the tour, the new image the Prince was creating for himself emerges clearly. Stanley noted:

> To me personally, I think H.R.H. has uniformly endeavoured, even at
> some loss to himself, to be as kind and considerate as he could be . . .
> However bored or annoyed he may be (and by particular individuals
> he has been sometimes, not without good reason) he has never shown
> it openly. Even in seeing antiquities, he will, from strangers, bear
> the longest expositions without appearance of fatigue . . . When the
> journey first began, I used to dread the formalities of interviews, etc.
> with high personages. I now rejoice in them, for in them he appears to
> the best advantage.

Stanley, perhaps unwittingly, highlighted the qualities Edward had been quietly acquiring and which had become apparent in his New World trips: the ability to listen (already noticed in Rome by Motley and Browning), sweetness and charm of manner (noticed by Disraeli), the cheerful self-discipline necessary to carry out lengthy public engagements, the ability to retain his own dignity and that pertaining to the occasion, without a trace of pomposity. Stanley noted that last quality with admiration: 'In Malta H.R.H. gave great satisfaction as usual ... I am struck with the ease with which he at once descends to our level, when all the show is over.' The Prince, in fact, had understood – and perhaps he was the first royal personage to do so – the value of 'public relations'. He was training himself, as a professional, for the years of public appearances ahead, for the profession of being King. Stanley had not quite appreciated fully, however, one of Edward's most endearing qualities, when he rather wistfully concluded his reflections: 'I shall not give him up, unless he gives me up.' Edward had a remarkable capacity for lasting friendships, and he never did 'give up' Stanley (who soon became Dean of Westminster and married General Bruce's sister, Lady Augusta).

Meanwhile, back in the gloomy mourning Court, the inconsolable Queen was clinging tenaciously to Albert's 'dearest wish' for the Danish marriage. When the Prince returned home on 13 June 1862, fit and healthy and 'much improved', very affectionate and kind to his little brothers and sisters for whom he had brought presents of Turkish finery for 'dressing-up' games, she was delighted when he also showed her some 'pretty things' he had bought in Paris for 'the young lady'. Arrangements immediately went ahead for the engagement. The public, who knew all about the short-list of candidates and had followed the whole affair with interest, already took it for granted that Alexandra was to be their Princess of Wales. Victoria set off for Coburg on a sentimental pilgrimage to Albert's childhood home. On the way she paused at Laeken, the palace-home outside Brussels of her uncle, King Leopold I of the Belgians. There, on 3 September, she interviewed Prince Christian and Princess Louise, parents of her prospective daughter-in-law, and had her first look at Alexandra, who wore a plain black dress, and had arranged her hair simply, with no ornaments, combed back from her forehead and with curls hanging over her shoulders. Victoria was delighted: 'Alexandra is lovely, such a beautiful, refined profile and quiet ladylike manners.'

As the Queen departed, well content, for Coburg, the Prince and his suite were setting out from England. But this time there was no Governor in the party. General Bruce had succumbed to a 'low Syrian fever', as it was called, at the end of the tour and died soon after reaching home. He was replaced in Edward's entourage, not by another Governor – by general agreement he was deemed to be now too 'grown-up' for this necessity – but by a Controller, General Sir William Knollys, a veteran soldier aged sixty-five. The Prince sincerely mourned his old Governor: 'It is really too sad to think that his end was caused by catching a fever on our tour which we all so thoroughly enjoyed ... I have lost a valuable friend.' He demurred at this new restraint imposed upon him, but was persuaded by his mother's anxious assurance that General Knollys was 'very fond of young people'. In fact it proved a happy choice; the new Controller was soon accepted by Edward as an agreeable companion. (General Knollys remained in the Prince's household for fifteen years; his son Francis soon joined him there as Edward's private secretary, a post he retained until Edward's death, and his daughter Charlotte became Lady-in-Waiting to Alexandra).

With his new Controller the Prince reached the Continent. In the Brussels hotel where his party, and the Danish family, were all staying, he formally asked Alexandra's father for her hand (afterwards commenting somewhat wryly to his mother: 'I don't think I ever saw anybody so much pleased as he was'). It was agreed between them that the proposal should take place at Laeken. Next morning, 9 September, they all drove out to the palace where, under the benevolent eye of King Leopold, Edward drew Alexandra away from the group admiring the gardens into the grotto and offered the seventeen-year-old girl 'his heart and hand'. 'She immediately said *yes*', the twenty-year-old suitor wrote to his mother, 'but I told her not to answer too quickly but to consider over it. She said she had long ago. I then asked her if

Engagement photograph of Edward and Alexandra, by King Leopold's photographers, Ghémar Frères, Brussels.
(National Portrait Gallery, London)

she liked me. She said *yes*. I then kissed her hand and she kissed me. We then talked for some time'. Back to King Leopold and the family went the young couple, to be showered with congratulations. After a few days in each other's company – although never permitted to be alone together – they separated, Alexandra returning home to prepare her trousseau, and Edward joining his mother in Coburg.

Except in one quarter, the announcement of the engagement was enthusiastically welcomed; the British public was delighted with the Danish connection, the Danes themselves overjoyed. The dissenting voice was that of Germany; a roar of rage greeted the engagement, which was seen as a political act linking Britain with Germany's enemy, Denmark. This reaction, although absolutely predictable, startled Victoria. Recovering quickly, she made plans to alleviate a possible political blunder: Alexandra was to visit her for three weeks in November, quite alone – without her parents or any Danish maids or ladies-in-waiting – to be inculcated with English ideas and viewpoints; as for the Prince, he was not to see his fiancée until the wedding and he was definitely not to visit Denmark to which he had been invited. Instead he was to be sent off on a Mediterranean cruise with his sister and brother-in-law, the Crown Princess and Prince of Prussia, who were being bitterly blamed for their part in arranging the Danish marriage. Protests against these arrangements were firmly dismissed by the Queen. Edward duly set off on his travels once more, with the result that on his twenty-first birthday he was 'somewhere in the Mediterranean', lying off Naples to be exact, a circumstance which aroused angry and critical comment at home where the public – in spite of the mourning for Albert still being observed – had been looking forward to a celebration with their Prince. In the Bay of Naples the British men-of-war were dressed overall and fired off rockets in the evening, while the masts of the *Osborne* were decked with crowns of evergreens. But it was a subdued occasion, and Edward wrote rather wistfully to a friend: 'The 9th was an important day for me this year . . . you can well imagine that I regretted very much not being at home on that day.' (Was it at this moment that the Prince decided that all his future birthdays would be celebrated in style?) Meanwhile, his young fiancée was sailing triumphantly through her ordeal at Osborne and Windsor, with Victoria becoming ever more fond of her future daughter-in-law: 'I can't say how I and we all love her. She is so good, so simple, unaffected, frank, bright and cheerful, yet so quiet and gentle that her companionship soothes me. Then how lovely! This jewel! She is one of those sweet creatures who seem to come from the skies to help and bless poor mortals and lighten for a time their path!' In this mood Victoria relented sufficiently to allow the young couple to meet for two days as they each travelled homewards.

On 3 December the Prince arrived back at Windsor to await his wedding, fixed for 10 March 1863. Cheerfully acquiescing in all his mother's arrangements for the occasion, he contemplated his life to come. Released almost simultaneously, by a curious stroke of fate, from the restraints and criticisms of his father and Governor and well able to find a code of conduct for his dealings with his mother, he had come of age with a self-confident, positive personality. Debonair and charming, he was about to possess a beautiful young wife and set up his own household in properties being prepared for him – Marlborough House in London and the country estate of Sandringham in Norfolk – while enjoying a handsome income. The future looked bright indeed.

4

FAMILY AFFAIRS AND FOREIGN RELATIONS

*T*HE COUNTRY had been deprived of a chance to celebrate the coming-of-age of the Prince, but it was determined to mark his marriage in proper style – and this in spite of Victoria's decision, for political and personal reasons, that the ceremonies should be as subdued as possible. The wedding itself was to take place in St George's Chapel, Windsor, an unpopular choice: Windsor was difficult to reach and the Chapel, even when crammed, could accommodate only about 900 guests. Demand for tickets was enormous and disappointed applicants were furious. London was also furious that neither its Westminster Abbey nor St Paul's was the chosen venue; over the past years the capital had seen few royal festivities to give its crowded population a jolly day's outing. But the Princess was due to pass through London on her way to Windsor, and the Corporation of London therefore resolved to give her a reception she would never forget. The huge sum of £40,000 was spent on decorations and illuminations; the city was resplendent with red cloth, banners, bunting and garlands of flowers. On Saturday 7 March 1863 the Royal Yacht *Victoria and Albert*, with Alexandra and her family on board, made its way slowly up the Thames in a tumult of welcome. Ships, dressed overall, sounded their hooters, guns boomed, church bells rang. At Gravesend the Prince, smartly dressed in grey trousers and blue frock-coat, leaped up the gangway and kissed his fiancée to rapturous applause and cheers. Alexandra wore a soft dove-grey gown, a violet mantle edged with fur, and a little white silk bonnet trimmed with pink roses which she had made herself. As the young couple stepped on to Gravesend pier, they were greeted by a group of pretty girls wearing white gowns and red cloaks (the Danish national colours) who scattered spring flowers at their feet. This charming welcome, loudly applauded by the excited watching crowds, was only the beginning of a triumphal day. A special train was waiting to take the party to the Bricklayers Arms Station in Southwark; the line was so crowded with well-wishers that the train could proceed only very slowly. Nor was progress any quicker when the party transferred to four carriages at Southwark. The little procession wended its slow way over London Bridge, through the City, along the Strand, Pall Mall, St James's Street, Piccadilly and Hyde Park to Paddington Station. The crowds, wearing wedding favours and many waving Danish flags, were immense. The police could not hold them back and the cordons were broken again and again. In a state of wild excitement everyone waited to catch a glimpse of the Life Guards escorting the carriages. As they came into sight there was a roar of delight: 'Here she is!' 'Hats off!' 'Hurrah!', and the crowds surged round the open carriage in which sat the smiling Prince and Princess. It took four hours for the party to reach Paddington. From Slough to Windsor huge crowds cheered the young couple whose first public appearance together had unexpectedly developed into an overwhelming manifestation of popular acclaim. Not even the pouring rain in which they arrived at Windsor, to be greeted by the Household and family, could dampen their radiance. The Queen's greeting was affectionate but curtailed; overcome with emotion she retired sadly to her rooms and a lonely dinner. Alexandra, however, in a display of the tact and feeling which she would always use towards her mother-in-law, knocked gently on the Queen's door, peeped in and embraced her sympathetically. Victoria never forgot this loving gesture. In softened mood she took the young couple on the eve of the wedding into the Mausoleum at Frogmore where Albert was buried, joined their hands and, embracing them fondly, blessed them in the name of her dead husband.

The wedding day, 10 March 1863, dawned bright and fine at Windsor. Early morning frost and fog in London cleared quickly as special trains, crowded with gorgeously dressed wedding guests, steamed out of Paddington. Four carriage processions left the Castle for the Chapel, the royal guests, the royal family, then the bridegroom and finally the bride. The Queen had refused to take part in the processions or participate in the ceremony. Instead she chose to sit above, and almost out of sight of, the congregation in the Royal Closet. In this secluded eyrie she sat in her sombre black mourning dress and widow's

Edward and Alexandra dressed for their wedding.
(National Portrait Gallery, London; photograph by Mayall)

cap, with only the Garter sash and Star to add a touch of colour. But this gloomy effect was obliterated by the brilliance of the congregation. All the men were in uniform, all the ladies in full Court dress (without their trains) and smothered in diamonds (those of the Duchess of Westminster were valued at half a million pounds), the Beefeaters and heralds were in their colourful uniforms, the State trumpeters, heralding each procession and those of the clergy, were in cloth of gold. The Prince wore his General's uniform and his Garter Robes with gold collar. As he entered the Chapel and walked steadily down the aisle, his Cambridge Professor and friend, Charles Kingsley, noted with satisfaction his serious reverent dignity, while his companion of the Middle East trip, Arthur Stanley, asked himself in wonder: 'Can this be the boy of last year on the Nile? Can this be the frolicsome creature for whom all our anxiety was that this marriage should take place, and now at last it is come?' Edward's own thoughts, after bowing to his mother and positioning himself between his 'supporters' – his uncle Duke Ernest of Saxe-Coburg-Gotha and his brother-in-law the Crown Prince of Prussia – were probably on the late arrival of his bride. Alexandra, who was incurably unpunctual and never succeeded in eradicating this fault, kept the whole church waiting for ten minutes. Apart from a few glances up at his agitated mother, the Prince waited manfully. But his patience, and that of the congregation, was well rewarded when the bride entered, a vision of loveliness, on her father's arm.

Alexandra's dress was of white satin, with puffings of white tulle, garnishes of orange blossom and trimmings of Honiton lace worked in a pattern of roses, thistles and shamrocks (for patriotic reasons this had been preferred to a beautiful creation in Brussels lace offered by King Leopold of the Belgians). Her hair fell in loose ringlets over her bare shoulders, and she wore part of Edward's lavish wedding present of jewellery – a delicately looped necklace of pearls and diamonds, matching button ear-rings and a large pearl brooch with pendant drops. Her bridal bouquet of orange blossoms, white rosebuds, lily-of-the-valley and sprigs of myrtle, was set in a holder of pink crystal studded with emeralds, rubies and diamonds (the present of Maharajah Dhuleep Singh). As she glided gracefully down the aisle, her train of silver moire antique trimmed with lace, tulle and orange blossom was carried by eight bridesmaids. The clear notes of Jenny Lind, the famous coloratura soprano known as the 'Swedish Nightingale', rang through the chapel in the chorale 'This day with joyful heart and voice' for which Albert had composed the music, in her eyrie the Queen raised her eyes to heaven, six clergymen, including the Archbishop of Canterbury, performed the ceremony, and the artist William Powell Frith, tucked away in a convenient corner with his sketchbook, recorded the scene which Benjamin Disraeli, one of the guests, considered 'a fine affair, a thing to remember'. One member of the royal family did not consider it a 'fine affair', however. William, the four-year-old son of the Crown Princess of Prussia – who would become 'The Kaiser' of history – had no interest in his Uncle Edward's wedding and behaved badly. Dressed in Highland costume, he managed to prise the cairngorm jewel from the handle of his little dirk and threw it into the choir. Reprimanded by his young uncles Arthur and Leopold, who were similarly attired, he bit them both on their bare legs. But this slight contretemps did not mar the splendid ceremony.

As the wedded pair left the Chapel to return to the Castle, guns boomed out and church bells rang, as they were booming and ringing all over the country. Thirty-eight members of the royal family sat down to the wedding-breakfast in the dining room; other guests were accommodated in St George's Hall.

The Landing of Princess Alexandra at Gravesend, 7 March 1863, by Henry Nelson O'Neil, 1864.
(National Portrait Gallery, London)

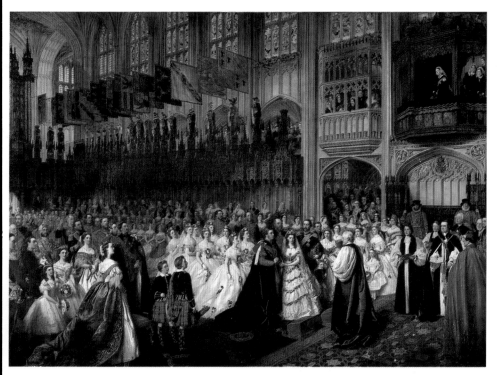

The Wedding of Edward and Alexandra, 10 March 1863, in St George's Chapel, Windsor, by
W P Frith.
(Royal Collection, St James's Palace. © Her Majesty The Queen)

49

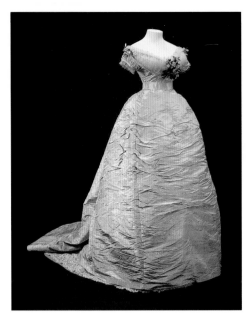

Alexandra's wedding dress.
(Museum of London)

Jenny Lind (1820–1887), the singer known as
'The Swedish Nightingale', who sang
Albert's chorale at Edward's wedding,
painted by Eduard Magnus. An 1864 replica
of the 1861 original.
(National Portrait Gallery, London)

London Bridge on the Night of the Marriage of The Prince and Princess of Wales, March 10, 1863,
by William Holman Hunt. The picture was exhibited in a London gallery and the royal couple
went to view it and meet the artist.
(Ashmolean Museum, Oxford)

Edward in his 30s. Chalk
drawing by G F Watts,
c.1874.
(National Portrait Gallery,
London)

William Ewart Gladstone (1809–1898) by
Sir John Everett Millais, 1879.
(National Portrait Gallery, London)

Benjamin Disraeli (1804–1881), Earl of
Beaconsfield, by Sir John Everett Millais,
1881.
(National Portrait Gallery, London)

Edward's sons, Albert Victor, aged 18, and George (later George V), aged 17, in midshipman's uniform, painted in 1882 when they returned home after three years at sea, by Carl Sohn the Younger.
(Royal Collection, St James's Palace. © Her Majesty The Queen)

Gunton Hall, as it looked when occupied by Edward and his family while Sandringham was being rebuilt. This elegant house was begun in 1742 and subsequently enlarged and embellished until Gunton Park became one of the most attractive estates in Norfolk.
(Mr Gavin Turner, private collection)

Edward's daughters. Left to right: Victoria (aged 15), Maud (aged 14), and Louise (aged 16), painted in 1883 by Sydney Prior Hall.
(National Portrait Gallery, London)

Sandringham House as it is today.
(Royal Collection, St James's Palace. © Her Majesty The Queen; photograph by Jarrold Colour Publishing)

A dinner-table, set for the dessert, at a party given in 1884 at Haddo House in Aberdeenshire, by the 1st Marquess of Aberdeen and Temair. The guests, who are being entertained at this stage of the dinner by a piper, include (right foreground) Mr Gladstone, and (left foreground) a friend of Edward, the politician Lord Rosebery. Painting by Alfred Edward Emslie. (National Portrait Gallery, London)

The State Chair used by Edward, when Prince of Wales, on official occasions. The chair is now at Grimsthorpe Castle, Lincolnshire. (By kind permission of the Baroness Willoughby de Eresby and the Trustees of the Grimsthorpe and Drummond Castle Trust; photograph courtesy of *The World of Interiors*, by James Mortimer)

London's first 'grand hotel', the Langham Hotel in Portland Place, opened by Edward in 1865. At that time the Langham was the largest building in London and soon became the most fashionable of meeting-places. It contained, as well as Italian-crafted mosaic floors, huge marble pillars and richly decorated ceilings, the then unheard-of features of air conditioning and hydraulic lifts.
(Contemporary print by courtesy of Mr Rudi Jagersbacher of the Langham Hilton)

The Building of the Victoria and Albert Museum, by Alex Jameson.
(By courtesy of the Board of Trustees of the Victoria & Albert Museum)

'The Uncle of Europe'. Edward stands in the centre of a huge gathering of his relations in a painting by L Tuxen to commemorate his mother's Golden Jubilee in 1887. (Royal Collection, St James's Palace. © Her Majesty The Queen)

Edward and Alexandra, after their wedding in their going-away clothes, posed round a bust of Albert, with Queen Victoria in full mourning dress. (Left to right) back row: Alexandra, Edward, Alice, her husband Louis of Hesse-Darmstadt; front row: Helena, Queen Victoria, Beatrice, Arthur and Victoria.
(National Portrait Gallery, London; photograph by Mayall)

The Queen, again refusing to participate, lunched alone in her rooms. But she reappeared at four o'clock to see the young couple off to Osborne House for their week's honeymoon, sharing in the tearful farewells and then running to a window under which their open carriage would pass. When they saw her, Edward stood up, Alexandra, snugly wrapped in a long mantle of ermine, waved, and both smiled lovingly at the lonely Queen. Excited and cheering crowds again accompanied the carriage to the station; the train stopped many times on the way to receive welcoming addresses and congratulations and it was late when the Prince and Princess of Wales reached Osborne House to start a new life together.

Meanwhile, back at Windsor, guests and sightseers were not faring so comfortably in their efforts to get back to London. Organisation had broken down under the sheer weight of numbers, and as train after train pulled into the station, thousands of people, including all the bejewelled ladies, fought to get on. Disraeli got a seat for his wife and then had to sit on her lap. Eventually they all got away to find London as chaotic as Windsor. Everything was decorated, St Paul's illuminated, all the theatres open and offering free seats, crowds milling around. London had been determined to celebrate the Prince's wedding and was doing so in fine style. Strolling through the City to view the decorations, the artist Holman Hunt noted how the dingy daytime buildings were transformed into a nocturnal fairy-land. Temple Bar was resplendent with gold and silver hangings. Masts on London Bridge were hung with big crimson banners showing the Danish elephant insignia, tripod braziers flared and everything was brilliantly lit up. The artist jotted down his impressions in his sketch book and later worked them up into a colourful canvas which captured the capital's festive mood. Nor was London alone in the desire to show approval of the wedding. Every town and village organised its own celebration; military parades, bell-ringing, concerts, public dinners – many given for the poor in the community – balls and fireworks were the order of the day. The song 'God Bless the Prince of Wales', written in the previous year by the Welsh composer Brinsley Richards, was now on everyone's lips, becoming a kind of supplementary national anthem. The *Welcome to Alexandra*, penned by the Poet Laureate, Alfred, Lord Tennyson, and beginning:

> Sea-king's daughter from over the sea,
> Saxon and Norman and Dane are we,
> But all of us Danes in our welcome of thee,
> Alexandra!

exactly epitomised the public's ecstatic welcome of, and admiration for, their new 'Danish Princess'. And the young composer Arthur Sullivan incorporated Danish airs into his *Princess of Wales' March*, performed for the first time at the Wedding Festival Concert at Crystal Palace.

Not only literary and musical offerings were forthcoming; presents flooded in from all quarters, especially for Alexandra. The Prince had already given his bride, whose parents were not wealthy, money for her trousseau and jewellery reputedly worth £15,000. Parliament voted her £10,000 'pin money', and the Danes did their Princess proud with a handsome dowry. Victoria's presents to her daughter-in-law included a diamond and opal cross, matching brooches and ear-rings and two elaborate Indian necklaces swagged with pearls, emeralds and rubies. The aged and ill King Frederick of Denmark countered with the 'Dagmar Necklace', a magnificent heirloom with 2,000 diamonds, 118 pearls and a replica of the eleventh century Dagmar Cross containing holy relics. All Edward's brothers and sisters gave personal presents, the Crown Princess of Prussia a gold locket, sister Alice and her husband, Louis of Hesse-Darmstadt a buckle-shaped turquoise bracelet with their initials entwined in diamonds, and the younger ones clubbed together to give an oval pendant of brilliants. To the generous family gifts filling her jewel case Alexandra was to add public offerings: London Corporation presented a diamond necklace sparkling with 32 brilliants and valued at £10,000, the Ladies of Liverpool a pearl necklace with a pendant diamond crown, the Ladies of Leeds a diamond bracelet and the Ladies of Manchester one of opals. The Highland Companies of the Edinburgh Rifle Volunteers struck an original note with their brooch of enamelled runic designs set with Scottish pearls, as did the Ladies of Ireland with their gift of exquisite lace. Interesting gifts to the couple included huge wrought-iron gates, to adorn their country house at Sandringham, from the Norfolk gentry, and a painting, *Head of a Young Girl* – a compliment to the Prince's interest in art – from his artist friend of Roman days, Frederic Leighton.

Alfred, Lord Tennyson (1809–1892),
Poet Laureate.
(National Portrait Gallery, London;
photograph attributed to James Mudd)

Head of a Young Girl, by Frederic
Leighton, given to Edward by the artist
as a wedding present.
(Royal Collection, St James's Palace.
© Her Majesty The Queen)

The young couple returned from their honeymoon, Edward 'so brightened up' and Alexandra 'so sweet and lovely', according to Victoria. Henceforth, over the next forty years of his 'in waiting' for the throne, Edward's life combined three elements: with startling rapidity, and ably assisted by Alexandra, the Prince invented, practised and perfected the mode of Society of which he became the image – the Edwardian Age had begun; alongside this element of his life ran the path of public duty, the appearances forced upon him by his mother's refusal to 'face the public' and which, as will be seen, assumed increasing importance as the years went by; and finally, the 'Foreign Relations', a designation which covers Edward's growing interest in Britain's foreign policy and the immense spread of his family connections.

During the Prince's years 'in waiting' Britain's foreign policy was largely based on her anxiety to preserve the 'balance of power' in Europe, while closely observing the great forces at work there, at first liberalism and nationalism, and later socialism. Two main areas of realignment of interests were emerging: the unification of Italy and, more complicated and far more menacing, the unification of Germany. On his travels Edward had witnessed, at a distance, some of the struggles in Italy. In England sympathy veered toward the gallant fighters for liberation and favoured a unified kingdom of North Italy comprising Piedmont, Florence and Modena. An enlarged version of this unification to include Naples and Sicily, produced by the exploits of the brave and picturesque Garibaldi and his Thousand, found acceptance. This unified kingdom was then transferred by Garibaldi to King Victor Emanuel II. Britain's non-intervention in these struggles won for her the friendship of the new kingdom. Early in 1864 Garibaldi was invited by the Duke of Sutherland to visit London privately. The Queen, and her Ministers, viewed the visit of this erstwhile 'rebel' and the popular enthusiasm it aroused with dismay. But Edward was made of sterner stuff and paid a call upon the Italian liberator. This brought a furious 'jobation' (the Prince's word for his mother's scolding) from the Queen on his 'incredible folly and imprudence'. Edward returned a calm reply to her angry letter: he pointed out that his visit had been quite private, described Garibaldi's appearance 'not tall, but dignified and noble', added disarmingly that Garibaldi had asked a great deal about the Queen, and that if she had seen him she 'would have been pleased with him as he is uncharlatanlike' and concluded with the unanswerable observation that he, the Prince, had always believed in the unity of Italy which was, after all, the Government's official policy.

The unification of Germany and her gradual emergence as a force to be reckoned with in Europe was an ongoing problem throughout all Edward's years as Prince of Wales, continuing during his reign and remaining to be handed on to his son and heir, George V. The foundations of this future area of conflict were being laid in September 1862, while Edward was proposing to Alexandra at the Palace of Laeken. King William of Prussia and his Parliament were deadlocked in a bitter dispute over the King's resolve to spend huge sums of money on army reform. Unable to extricate himself from an impossible position the King recalled his ambassador to France, Count von Bismarck, to assume overall control and dissolve parliament. Bismarck's ominous words, 'It is not with speeches or with parliamentary resolutions that the great questions of the day are decided . . . but with blood and iron', ushered in an uneasy relationship with the rest of Europe. Bismarck's policies soon impinged upon the Prince's married life. On 15 November 1863 old King Frederick of Denmark died and was succeeded by Alexandra's father as King Christian IX. Exactly as had been foretold Prussia chose this moment to put forward its claims to the Duchies of Schleswig and Holstein, then under Danish rule. Recruiting Austria as a war-partner, Prussian troops were soon on the march and the Duchies were annexed. In spite of widespread public sympathy for 'poor little Denmark' Britain played her non-intervention card. Divided loyalties in the royal family caused uproar at Windsor. Victoria, with her pro-German daughter whose husband, the Crown Prince, was with the Prussian army, and her Danish daughter-in-law who shouted angrily at the dinner table 'The Duchies belong to Papa!', finally forbade any discussion on the subject. Edward, who stoutly stood by his wife, reflected the opinion of most of the population and of the Government Opposition in denouncing the policy of neutrality and clamouring for the British fleet to be sent to the Baltic. But it was all to no avail. Prussia had taken her first step towards German unification, and Alexandra conceived an undisguised hatred for all things German which lasted throughout her life.

During this period of hostilities the Prince became a father. Alexandra had suffered an agitated pregnancy, worrying about her country and crying herself to sleep night after night. Since the baby was not expected until March, the couple decided to have a short holiday at Frogmore House near Windsor early in January 1864. The weather was very cold and the party went skating every day. On 8 January they went to Virginia Water; Edward played in an ice-hockey game, Alexandra enjoyed being pushed about on the ice in a chair fitted with runners, and while a band played the party ate a picnic lunch. In the afternoon Alexandra felt a little unwell and, while the ice-hockey game continued, she and her Lady of the Bedchamber, Lady Macclesfield, returned to Frogmore. As the ladies reached the house, Alexandra's labour began. Fortunately Lady Macclesfield was herself the mother of a large family and kept her head admirably. Getting the Princess to bed, she sent servants running to find Dr Brown, a local Windsor doctor who in the past had attended the Queen, and other servants to buy flannel and cotton-wool at the local draper's shop, since nothing was ready in the house. She telegraphed to London for the doctors who had been retained for the event and to the Home Secretary whose presence was essential at the birth of an eventual heir to the throne – and even found time to get one of her own flannel petticoats ready to receive the baby as it was born. In all this bustle and excitement the Prince came home after his match and was astounded to find his wife in labour. Rushing to her he held her hand and encouraged her. Dr Brown had still not been found; more servants, and some of the guests in the party, joined the search. At last he galloped up to the house. Twenty minutes later he and Lady Macclesfield delivered a baby boy weighing under 4 pounds. Albert Victor Christian Edward was wrapped in the flannel petticoat and cotton-wool and put in a basket beside a big fire, watched by his proud, and exhausted, nineteen-year-old mother and twenty-two-year-old father. (The Home Secretary did not arrive in time, but Lord Granville, the Lord President, fortuitously

Edward, Alexandra and their first-born, Albert Victor.
(National Portrait Gallery, London; photograph by Vernon Heath, 1864)

61

hunting at Windsor, stood in for him.) When Victoria, at Osborne, received the news, she was furious and the young parents were subjected to a royal 'jobation': there had been carelessness, too much gallivanting and Alexandra had not taken care of herself. In the event, however, all the children of the Prince and Princess of Wales were premature – 'these poor, frail, little fairies' their grandmother commented sadly. By the age of twenty-eight Edward was the father of five: his second son, George, was born in June 1865, at Marlborough House as were his three daughters, Louise in February 1867, Victoria in July 1868 and Maud in November 1869. (A sixth baby, Alexander John, born at Sandringham on 6 April 1871, died the following day.)

But there was to be no retreat into purely domestic life for the Prince. Alexandra's brother, a seventeen-year-old naval cadet, was invited to become King of Greece (King Otho had been expelled after a revolution in 1862 and the throne was vacant); backed by Britain he accepted and became King George I of the Hellenes in 1863. Later Alexandra's sister Dagmar became engaged to Alexander, son of the Russian Czar (on becoming Czarina in 1881 she adopted the name of Marie). These events, serving in some measure as a counterbalance to German predominance, widened the already extensive network of Edward's 'foreign relations'.

In September 1864 the young couple, overcoming Victoria's stiff resistance, travelled to Denmark to show off their baby son to Alexandra's family. While there, they accepted an invitation from Sweden's King Charles XV to stay in his castle at Stockholm. This enjoyable visit, which included an exciting elk hunt, provoked a stream of angry letters and telegrams from Victoria, already alarmed at Denmark's rapturous welcome and furious at this contact with her neighbour. Edward, proving himself a better diplomatist than his mother, sent a dignified reply: that there was no need to annoy Sweden by rejecting the invitation, that he, the Prince, would always try to comply with his mother's wishes, 'but if I am not to use my own discretion we had better give up travelling'. Victoria riposted with strict orders to visit German relatives on the way home to show the world, as she put it, that Edward was not only the son-in-law of the King of Denmark but 'the child of his parents'. As might have been expected these visits were not particularly successful, since the Crown Prince of Prussia had the tactlessness to greet Alexandra wearing a military decoration he had won in the war against her father. These family squabbles grumbled on, exacerbated by the engagement of Edward's sister Helena to Christian, younger brother of the Duke of Augustenburg who had supported Prussia against Denmark, and punctuated by periodical reconciliations. Visits by the Prince and Princess to Osborne and Windsor were welcomed by Victoria, although in 1865 she was despairing over their 'two tiny little boys', Albert Victor and George, and finding Alexandra 'pale and thin'. And on 26 August of the same year, Victoria gathered eight of her nine children about her at Coburg for the ceremonial unveiling in the market square of a statue of her beloved Albert.

But storm clouds were gathering over Europe as Bismarck prepared his next move. In mid-June 1866 Prussia made war against her one-time ally Austria, and on 3 July beat her so decisively at the Battle of Sadowa (Königsgratz – later Hradec Kralové) in Bohemia, that Austria and her partners, the southern German states, had to surrender. The Seven Week War, as it came to be called, ended on 22 August with the Treaty of Prague by which Prussia gained all she had sought: her boundaries were greatly extended, she took in the territory of Hanover, Hesse-Cassel became a German province, the port of Kiel was

Statue of Prince Albert, depicted in Garter Robes, in the marketplace at Coburg, unveiled in August 1865 in the presence of Edward, his mother and his brothers and sisters.
(Fremdenverkehrs- und Kongressbetrieb der Stadt Coburg; photograph by Balthasar Heinlein, Ahorn)

earmarked as the base for Germany's future navy and Bismarck, all-triumphant, made himself Chancellor of a North German Confederation from which Austria was excluded. Britain watched these events with dismay but remained neutral. On a personal level, the royal family was again bitterly divided, with emotions ranging from anger against Prussia's Crown Prince and Princess to pity for dispossessed German relatives who included the King of Hanover, Edward's brother-in-law Louis of Hesse-Darmstadt and Alexandra's maternal uncle of Hesse-Cassel. Only Edward, of all the family including his mother, would appear to have taken a cool look at Prussia's aggression and to have suggested a feasible political deterrent, namely an alliance between Britain and France. In long conversations with the French ambassador in London the Prince put forward this eminently sensible idea which was duly reported to the French government. (But the envisaged *Entente* was not to become reality for some forty years.)

By the autumn, with Prussia's aggrandisement reluctantly accepted in Europe, Edward's attention was directed to Russia, where he was invited to attend the wedding of Alexandra's sister Dagmar to the Czar's son Alexander. Relations between Britain and Russia had not been overly cordial since the Crimean War and the Government was cautiously working towards a better understanding. The Prince obligingly declared: 'I should be only too happy to be the means in any way of promoting the *entente cordiale* between Russia and my own country', and, 'I am a very good traveller, so that I should not at all mind the length of the journey', and set off at the end of October 1866 (Alexandra, pregnant with her third child, was unable to accompany him). On the way, yielding to his mother's pleadings and his own genuine affection for his brother-in-law, he made it up with the Crown Prince of Prussia who was also invited to the Russian wedding. Edward, who celebrated his twenty-fifth birthday in St Petersburg, was received with gratifying attention. The entertainments offered to him included military parades, a ball at which he wore his kilt, a ceremonial banquet and fete in Moscow, and a thrilling wolf hunt (the bag was seven wolves).

On his return to London family problems replaced foreign ones. His wife had contracted rheumatic fever, their third child Louise was born prematurely on 20 February 1867 and Alexandra made a very slow recovery from post-natal infections, remaining afflicted for the rest of her life with a slight limp, due to a stiffened leg, and increasing deafness (an inherited disability). By August Edward had decided that she might benefit from treatment at the famous Spa Baths at Wiesbaden and led, to this charming resort, a cavalcade consisting of Alexandra in her wheel-chair, their three little children, two doctors, the equerries and twenty-five servants. A house was rented and the treatment began. But 'foreign relations' intruded even into this family interlude. Prussia's King William sent a telegram expressing his desire to pay a call on the Princess. This tactless action had the obvious result. Alexandra exploded with rage and refused to see the King. Tiresome scenes followed, letters and telegrams flew back and forth, and the Prince had his hands full trying to placate his angry wife and reconcile her to the peremptory orders of Victoria and the Crown Princess. Writing diplomatically to his mother, Edward put forward an interesting 'Edwardian' view of the difference between the sexes: 'A lady may have feelings which she cannot repress, while a man *must* overcome them.' But even this gallant interpretation of Alexandra's state of mind did not suffice to satisfy the Queen: Edward's wife must not let her private feelings interfere with her 'duties'. After a particularly trying discussion, cut short by Alexandra hobbling out of the room with the aid of her walking stick, Edward put an end to the affair. He wrote a telegram inviting the King to breakfast next day, showed it to his wife and quickly sent it off. The household waited in trepidation for the morning. But when the King arrived, escorted by the Prince, everyone was relieved to see Alexandra behave with civility. The King was pleased and insisted on staying for luncheon.

A period of uneasy truce followed, in Europe and in the royal family. In January 1869 Edward met Bismarck for the first time. The occasion was a social one; the Prince and Princess were passing through Berlin on their way to a Nile cruise to restore Alexandra's poor health after the birth of her fourth child. The Prussian King held a special Chapter to invest the Prince with the Order of the Black Eagle; Bismarck, Count von Molke, Chief of Staff of the Prussian army, and the veteran Field-Marshal von Wrangel were all present, and Edward therefore found himself conversing with the leading architects of Prussian aggrandisement.

Edward's political education was proceeding apace; to the inherent qualities which he had displayed during his New World tours – namely his ability to get on with all types of people, his charm of manner, his talent for public appearances and above all his readiness to listen to the views of others – was now being added an accumulating wealth of experience acquired through personal encounters with the leading figures of the day. The Prince, in fact, was fitting himself for the role of a 'roving ambassador' or perhaps rather as a kind of Edwardian counterpart of today's participants in the face-to-face confrontations of world leaders. But his suitability for this role was never fully recognised, either by most successive British governments or, more importantly, by the Queen. The dead hand of Albert lay heavy on the Prince's prospects of being given a political role, or even of being gradually initiated into the mysteries of monarchical government. The Queen's opinion of her heir remained congealed in the dying Albert's critical and reproachful attitude to his adolescent son. To the widowed mother her eldest son was 'nice, kind,

The Kurhaus (Spa Baths) at Wiesbaden in the 1860s. Edward took Alexandra here for treatment in 1867. (By kind permission of the Stadtarchiv, Wiesbaden)

Edward and Alexandra and their young family at Abergeldie in Scotland in autumn 1868: (left to right) George (future George V), Alexandra holding baby Victoria, Louise, Albert Victor and Edward. (National Portrait Gallery, London; photograph by W and D Downey)

affectionate', 'a most loving son', but never the political partner to take Albert's place. Edward's attitude to world events was never insular; his interests could be called European, in the widest sense of the word. Perhaps for this reason, although virtually without influence in his own country, his

65

opinion and influence were sought abroad. And it would seem that it was from this viewpoint that he closely observed Prussia's growing importance.

The paths of the Prince and Bismarck were to cross many times. Was Edward taken in by the all-powerful Chancellor's courtesy at their first meeting in 1869? He had already, two years earlier, written to Mrs Bruce, widow of his old 'Governor', expressing his fears that 'future troubles are brewing between France and Prussia'. But even he could not have foreseen the magnitude of Bismarck's next exploit. The throne of Spain having become vacant through the expulsion of Queen Isabella, Prussia put up one of her King's relatives as a candidate. France took fright, protested vigorously and after some confused diplomatic wrangling rashly declared war on Prussia on 15 July 1870. Britain, under Gladstone's government, immediately declared her neutrality and the royal family was again divided in its loyalties. The Queen and the Crown Princess were strongly pro-Prussian; the Crown Prince was again fighting in the German army; Alexandra's father toyed with the idea of taking Denmark into the war as an ally of France, and the Prince himself, torn between his ties with Germany and his love for France, vainly offered his services as a mediator for peace. Events moved swiftly; the German army inflicted a series of stunning defeats on France at Worth, Metz and Sedan. By 1 September the French Emperor Napoleon III was a prisoner; by 4 September France had formed the Third Republic and the German armies were advancing rapidly on Paris. Eventually the besieged city had to capitulate, France gave up Alsace and Lorraine to her conqueror, and in the Palace of Versailles King William had himself proclaimed as Emperor of the newly established German Empire, of which Bismarck became Chancellor. Prussia, indeed, had 'swallowed up everything' and thereby expanded herself into a formidable Empire, a transformation which overthrew the 'balance of power' in Europe and was to have far-reaching and ominous effects.

One effect became apparent almost immediately in England. Republican sentiments had been rumbling underground for some time; inflamed by the fall of the French Emperor, the proclamation of the Republic and the heroic defence of Paris by the Communards, these feelings burst into the open. Republican clubs sprang up in London and the big towns; the Government grew increasingly nervous as criticism of the monarchy intensified. At this precarious moment, Edward fell gravely ill with typhoid fever just after celebrating his thirtieth birthday at Sandringham in November 1871. Members of the royal family, including the Queen, flocked to his bedside. The Prince's life hung virtually by a thread; raving in delirium he shouted, laughed, whistled and hurled his pillows about before falling back exhausted while his helpless doctors stood round him. Bulletins were issued every day, one day as many as five were sent out. Sandringham was surrounded by well-wishers and reporters waiting to rush the latest bulletins to the telegraph office. The public eagerly read every scrap of news; by 10 December they were being prepared for the worst. The fact that Albert had died of the same disease on 14 December was in everyone's minds and, sure enough, on the night of 13–14 December the crisis came. In a last, despairing effort one of the doctors ordered that the sinking patient be rubbed down with 'old champagne brandy'; after this treatment Edward fell into a natural sleep. When he woke, very thirsty, his brother Alfred offered him a glass of ale. Gulping it down, he demanded another; he had turned the corner.

The delighted public lapped up the story of the dreaded 14 December and the glasses of ale. They were rewarded for their sympathy by an open letter of thanks from the Queen and by a grand Thanksgiving Ceremony in London on 27 February 1872. The Prince, still thin and drawn, and his mother rode in an open carriage accompanied by London's Lord Mayor and an escort of cavalry via the Strand and Fleet Street to St Paul's, where some 13,000 spectators had packed themselves in, for the service, and returned via Holborn and Oxford Street through enormous cheering crowds, a scene described by Poet Laureate Tennyson (in the Epilogue to his *Idylls of the King*): 'And London rolled one tide of joy through all Her trebled millions'. Two months later Arthur Sullivan's musical thank-offering for Edward's recovery, his *Te deum laudamus*, was performed with a huge choir and orchestra to great acclaim at Crystal Palace. To the amazement of observers this unexpected flood of sympathy for, and loyalty to, the throne, occasioned by the Prince's illness, swept away most of the republican agitation. The freely expressed sentiment 'What a sell for Dilke [Sir Charles Dilke, the Radical politician] this illness has been!', summed up the situation; the movement never regained its early momentum.

The Prince, with considerable political acumen, was soon to draw Dilke into his social circle and make a friend of him, and he used a similarly diplomatic approach to his mother's two political giants, Gladstone and Disraeli. Unlike Victoria, who could not conceal her personal dislike of Liberal Gladstone while openly favouring Conservative Disraeli, Edward counted both men as his friends and maintained a non-party basis in his dealings with them. His understanding of the role of the constitutional monarch would therefore appear to have developed early during his period 'in waiting'. Both these Prime Ministers tried to persuade the Queen to admit her heir into her political confidence and share her duties and responsibilities with him. Both failed. Although the Prince, from time to time, received edited reports of Cabinet proceedings, not until 1892 was he given the golden key, made for his father, to open the boxes of the government department which interested him most, namely the Foreign Office. Edward's foreign policy notions often coincided with those of Disraeli, and in one interesting area he may have anticipated the statesman. On his cruise up the Nile with Alexandra in 1869 he inspected work being done on the almost-completed Suez Canal, met the

Sir Charles Wentworth Dilke (1843–1911), the Republican and radical politician who became Edward's friend, painted by George Frederic Watts, 1873. (National Portrait Gallery, London)

French designer Ferdinand de Lesseps and expressed his great regret that Britain had missed her chance to take part in this major enterprise, which he later described as 'our highway to India'. His delight, therefore, when Disraeli astutely acquired a major stake in the Canal in 1875 was immense and found expression in a warm letter of congratulations: 'In the eyes of the whole world it is a step which has met with the highest approval . . . on all sides I hear what an excellent effect it has had on the continent.'

The following year Disraeli and the Prince again pursued the same political line. Trouble erupted when Turkey's Christian subjects in the Balkans rebelled; her harshly repressive measures shocked British public opinion. Fears that Russia would intervene, especially after the assassination of Turkey's Sultan, prompted proposals from France and Britain for a conference of the Great Powers in Constantinople to solve the Balkan problem. This broke up inconclusively and Russia declared war on Turkey in April 1877. Gladstone, in Opposition, agitated vociferously for Russia; Prime Minister Disraeli came down eventually on the side of Turkey, 'The Sick Man of Europe'. In this policy he was strongly backed by both Victoria and the Prince, and this in spite of close family connections with Russia – Edward's brother Alfred had recently married the Czar's daughter Marie, and Alexandra's sister had married the Czar's son. All through the Balkan crisis Disraeli kept in close touch with Edward, accepting his suggestion that Britain's representative at the Constantinople Conference should on the way visit the capitals of the four Great Powers – France, Germany, Austria and Italy – and take soundings of their views. Disraeli defended this early example of 'shuttle diplomacy' when he told the British envoy:

> The Prince of Wales is a thorough man of the world and knows all these individuals personally. You must remember we suffer from a feeble and formal diplomacy and that there has been little interchange of thought between the English Government and foreign powers. I agree with the Prince and think it highly desirable that at this moment our communications with the Powers should be lifted out of the slough of despond they have so long grovelled in.

By January 1878 Britain was on the brink of war, with the Prince urging: 'Depend upon it, words not backed up by deeds now are perfectly useless.' Seven thousand Indian troops were ordered to Malta, and the Mediterranean Fleet was sent off to Constantinople. A new song swept the nation and 'Jingoism' was born:

> We don't want to fight; but, by Jingo, if we do,
> We've got the ships, we've got the men, we've got the money too.

In the event these warlike 'deeds' sufficed to halt Russia. An armistice was signed and a Congress of the Great Powers proposed to settle the Balkan affair once and for all. Bismarck now threw his weight in, suggested Berlin as the venue and himself as the 'honest broker'. Who was to be the British represent-ative at this important meeting? In Edward's view the only candidate was Disraeli himself. He wrote urgently to the Queen:

> It strikes me more forcibly than ever that the Prime Minister is not only *the* right man to represent us at a Congress, but the *only* man who can go – as he would show Russia and the other Powers that we were really in earnest, and that Lord B. [Disraeli had accepted the title of Lord

Beaconsfield] was himself going to carry the Policy we had laid down in Parliament and stick to it to the last . . . do let me implore you to urge Lord B. to go – as it is a matter of such vital importance to our Country and dignity that we come out of the difficulty masters of the situation.

He ended with the revealing remark: 'Excuse me having written on the subject, but it is one in which I take such interest, that I could not help doing so.' Disraeli, although in poor health, did go to the Congress of Berlin and he wrote to Edward triumphantly on 22 June on the result of his tussle with Bismarck: 'Dearest Prince, I am almost ashamed to send you this not only illegible but illiterate scrawl . . . Turkey is in my pocket . . . Russia is now, more hopelessly than ever, excluded from the Mediterranean', adding jocularly that Bismarck had drunk champagne while he (Disraeli) had to smoke a great deal, 'but if I had not I should not have gained many points'. On 6 July he confidentially informed the Prince that he had acquired Cyprus for Britain: 'we enter into a defensive alliance with Turkey as respects all her Asiatic dominions, and with the consent of the Sultan we occupy the island of Cyprus. It is the key of Asia and is near to Egypt. Malta is too far as a military base for these purposes . . . In great haste, ever Sir and dear Prince . . .'. The Prince's fruitful association with Disraeli reveals a not always sufficiently appreciated side to his character. Like the veteran statesman, he held 'large views' (Victoria's description of her favoured Minister) and saw Britain not as a little country in splendid isolation, but as one of the Great Powers of Europe, whose influence rested not only on royal family alliances but on her expanding trade and colonial – later imperial – interests. Under Disraeli's guidance these 'European and Imperial' sentiments were, paradoxically enough, those of the Queen herself. But Disraeli's death in 1881 destroyed any chance of mother and son becoming political partners. The Prince would have to wait for another twenty years before he could contribute properly to an area of such interest to him.

From the Congress of Berlin, Disraeli was said to have brought back 'Peace with Honour' and for the next thirty-six years, up to the outbreak of the First World War, Europe did enjoy a somewhat uneasy respite. But always in the background and looming larger and larger as the years went by, was the ominous presence of a strong Germany, which increasingly occupied Edward's attention. In March 1888 his brother-in-law the Crown Prince became Emperor. The Prince's hopes, however, that a more liberal regime might be inaugurated in Germany were of short duration. The reign of the new Emperor, who was dying of cancer of the throat, lasted only a hundred days. He was succeeded as Emperor by his son William, the little boy who had behaved so badly at his Uncle Edward's wedding and who, under Bismarck's guiding hand, had developed into an arrogant, overbearing and ambitious young man, became the new 'Kaiser' – as he was popularly known in Britain. From this moment on Edward's troubled relationship with his nephew reflected Britain's uneasy preoccupation with the emerging German Empire. Within two years the Kaiser had thrown off Bismarck's tutelage, abruptly dismissing him on 19 March 1890. The Prince happened to be in Berlin at the time and promptly paid a visit of condolence to the old Chancellor whom he found seething with rage and resentment. Bismarck was far from popular in Europe, but the prospect of a rash and reckless, militaristic and autocratic young ruler in sole charge of a powerful Germany could only dismay her neighbours. Britain's policy of being both firm and conciliatory was pursued

'Dropping the Pilot': *Punch* magazine's cartoon depicting the abrupt dismissal of the German chancellor Bismarck by Kaiser William in March 1890.
(Reproduced by permission of *Punch*)

DROPPING THE PILOT.

with indifferent success. The Prince, representing his mother, had to pay many visits to Germany; the Kaiser, for his part, insisted on visiting England where Edward had to receive him. And all the time Germany's armed forces, and especially her navy, were being built up. That the Kaiser was obsessed with ambition to make Germany a great naval power became apparent at a naval review at Spithead in August 1889 where the honorary dignity of British Admiral was bestowed upon him. Receiving this honour with ecstatic delight – 'Fancy wearing the same uniform as Nelson!' – he then proceeded not only to shower unwanted advice and suggestions on his astonished naval hosts but also to interrogate them closely on detailed technical matters. Back home in Berlin he continued to send unasked-for naval advice, 'the humble opinion of a simple Admiral of the Fleet', to his irritated grandmother and uncle. Edward indeed, had to endure many pinpricks and insults from his obstreperous nephew, and as the century drew to a close, relationships, both family and political, became ever more strained.

Meanwhile the Prince's own family was growing up, with all the attendant pleasures and worries of bringing up children. Edward was a kind and indulgent father and Alexandra, above all else, a doting, and somewhat possessive, mother. The Prince, perhaps remembering his own weary and anxious days in the schoolroom, did not subject his five children to a similarly severe regime. They were allowed to run wild to some extent – Victoria labelled them 'ill-trained' – and schooling was minimal. In the early days their health was a matter of concern and they were often sickly, 'most wretched' according to their critical grandmother, 'excepting Georgie who is always merry and rosy'. 'Georgie', the future George V, was a year younger than his brother, yet more advanced in every aspect. Albert Victor, the Prince's heir,

Edward and his family in 1884. Alexandra (back row, second left) stands beside her younger son George (first left); her hand rests on the shoulder of her elder son Albert Victor (seated centre front row).
(Museum of London; photograph by Russell & Sons)

was handsome and good-natured, but even his indulgent parents had to recognise at last that his backwardness, lethargy and dawdling ways could never be rectified. In 1879, after long consultations with the Queen, the Prince decided to send his two sons off as midshipmen on a world cruise which lasted for three years. On their return in 1882 George continued his naval career, while strenuous, though unsuccessful, efforts were made by Edward to prepare his elder son for the position he would eventually have to occupy.

By 1891 the Prince had come to the conclusion that what his son needed was 'a good sensible wife with some considerable character'. His choice fell upon the young Princess May of Teck, daughter of Victoria's cousin; the engagement followed and the wedding was arranged for 27 February 1892. But fate decreed otherwise: Albert Victor fell victim to the influenza epidemic sweeping the country, developed inflammation of the lungs and died, aged twenty-eight, at Sandringham on 14 January. The grief of the bereaved parents was acute. Alexandra was heart-broken; Edward's sad words to the Archbishop of Canterbury, 'Our beloved son is happier now than if he were exposed to the miseries and temptations of this world,' reveal his awareness of his son's failings but also bear witness to his deep attachment to his first-born. The Prince's thoughts soon turned to his intended daughter-in-law, and he wrote to his mother: 'It is hard that poor little May should virtually become a widow before she is a wife.' The Queen's suggestion that George should

'Four Generations' (Queen Victoria, Edward, his son George – later George V – and George's son Edward – later Edward VIII and Duke of Windsor), painted in 1897 by Sir William Quiller Orchardson. On 19 June 1907 Edward VII strongly recommended to his Prime Minister the bestowal of a knighthood on 'W.Q. Orchardson who painted *Four Generations*', and the artist received this honour.
(National Portrait Gallery, London)

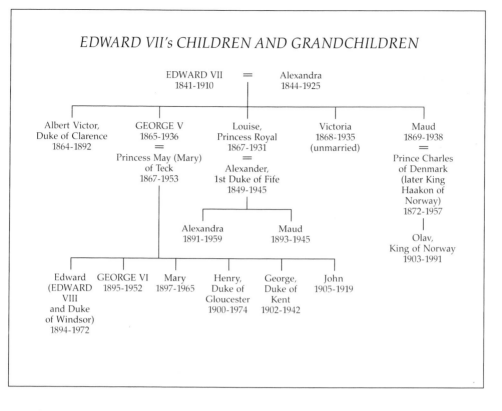

EDWARD VII's CHILDREN AND GRANDCHILDREN

EDWARD VII = Alexandra
1841-1910   1844-1925

Albert Victor,   GEORGE V   Louise,   Victoria   Maud
Duke of Clarence   1865-1936   Princess Royal   1868-1935   1869-1938
1864-1892   =   1867-1931   (unmarried)   =
   Princess May (Mary)   =   Prince Charles
   of Teck   Alexander,   of Denmark
   1867-1953   1st Duke of Fife   (later King
   1849-1945   Haakon of
   Norway)
   1872-1957

Alexandra   Maud
1891-1959   1893-1945

Olav,
King of Norway
1903-1991

Edward   GEORGE VI   Mary   Henry,   George,   John
(EDWARD   1895-1952   1897-1965   Duke of   Duke of   1905-1919
VIII   Gloucester   Kent
and Duke   1900-1974   1902-1942
of Windsor)
1894-1972

marry May had already occurred to the public and was considered the ideal solution. Their engagement in May and wedding in July of 1893 were greeted with general rejoicing. The young couple settled down in York Cottage on the Sandringham Estate, and George gave up his naval career to be prepared for his new role as the Prince's heir. Their first baby, a boy (afterwards Edward VIII and then Duke of Windsor) was born in June 1894. Public excitement was generated by the realisation that never before had three direct heirs to the throne, and the reigning sovereign, all been alive together. This happy coincidence engendered a spate of 'Four Generations' photographs and pictures, a fashion which never lost its popularity.

This little boy was the Prince's third grandchild. He had already become a grandfather at the early age of forty-nine, when his daughter Louise, married to the Earl (later Duke) of Fife, gave birth to her first daughter in May 1891. Edward was eventually to count a total of nine grandchildren: George and May had six children, Louise had two and Maud, who married her cousin Prince Charles of Denmark (the couple were later invited to become King and Queen of Norway), had one son (Victoria remained unmarried). But as his years 'in waiting' rolled steadily on to the end of the century, it was rather as the 'Uncle of Europe' that the Prince was becoming known, a title which aptly combined his ever-widening interest, and experience, in the political happenings on the Continent with the equally increasing network of his family connections.

5

EDWARDIAN SOCIETY AND ITS CREATOR

*W*HEN DISRAELI described the Prince as 'one who really has seen everything and knows everybody', he was referring not only to Edward's European interests, travels and family connections, but also to his role as the leader of English Society. Before his twenty-first birthday Edward had already created an image for himself. He then had to set about creating his background, the stage on which he would be the leading actor for the rest of his life, and which will always be associated with his name – Edwardian Society – and the opportunity to do this came with his marriage in 1863. On that occasion the Prince's financial position was considered by the House of Commons. To his annual revenue, amounting to some £50,000, from the Duchy of Cornwall, Parliament decided to add £40,000; with some other additions this brought his annual income to around £100,000. Edward also entered into possession of his town and country residences: Marlborough House in Pall Mall, and the house and estate of Sandringham in Norfolk which had been purchased by Albert with his son's revenues for £220,000. The Prince, therefore, provided with his income, his houses and his beautiful, young and pleasure-loving partner, was poised to inaugurate his own royal lifestyle and dispel the gloom of the Windsor Court.

The Court of Victoria and Albert had been essentially a domestic one. This sprang, in part, from a deliberate policy. Victoria was determined to wipe out the memory of the extravagant and loose-living Court of George IV. After her marriage to Albert and the regular arrival of their children, this objective merged with the aim of demonstrating to the public the virtues of family life. Court life, therefore, except for the occasional visit of a foreign head of state, was quiet and staid. Albert's basic condemnation of the aristocracy as 'frivolous' was soon shared by Victoria, and their social circle included only a very small section of the 'nobility', a few selected officials and their own kinsfolk. After Albert's death this circle became even more restricted, the Court moved away from London when Victoria retreated to out-of-town Windsor, remote Balmoral and rather inaccessible Osborne, and Buckingham Palace was well-nigh abandoned. The time was ripe for Society to have a new leader and Edward, stepping into the vacuum created by his mother, quickly assumed this role.

Returning from their honeymoon at Osborne, the Prince and Princess visited Victoria at Windsor and then, on 19 March, took up residence in their London home, Marlborough House. This was the signal for a 'season' during the summer of 1863 such as London had not seen for years – a royal public honeymoon lasting for months. Edward escorted his wife, glittering in her diamonds, to balls, parties, banquets, dances, receptions; in spite of Alexandra's pregnancy the whirl of amusements did not slacken all year. This provoked many 'jobations' from Windsor: the Prince 'goes on going out every night until she [Alexandra] becomes a Skeleton'; they were 'nothing but puppets, running about for show all day and night'. One of Victoria's objections centred on her son's innovative adoption of the practice of 'dining out' at other people's houses which, except for a few privileged establishments, she considered undesirable. Her reasons for this were mixed: her dislike of the 'frivolous' aristocracy, fears for the stability of the monarchy,

Edward's London residence, Marlborough House, in the 1860s.
(By courtesy of the Board of Trustees of the Victoria & Albert Museum)

distrust of the new classes coming up into Society, and anxiety about the example this practice, and the general pursuit of pleasure, would give to the 'Lower Orders'. But the Prince, even at the age of twenty-one, had already become aware of the changing spirit of the times and the rise of the upper-middle classes and understood the advisability of admitting to Society men and women hitherto excluded. Disliking arrogance and snobbery, he firmly believed that what was important was not a man's birth, but his character and achievements – rank alone was not sufficient to make a man a personage in his eyes. Under his leadership, through the years Society widened to embrace industrialists, bankers, politicians, lawyers, doctors, artists, actors and actresses, writers and sportsmen.

Edward was also finding a way of dealing with his mother which he was to practice throughout all his years 'in waiting'. This was to avoid as far as possible face-to-face encounters – very feasible once the Prince was independent and had his own establishments – and instead to exchange views by letter. This was, in any case, Victoria's preferred method of communication with her Ministers and officials of her household, particularly so in her secluded widowhood. Most of Victoria's 'jobations' were couched in written terms, as were her son's polite replies, disclaimers and suggestions. To modern readers this method of communication between a monarch and her heir might indicate a cold relationship. As monarch Victoria excluded the Prince politically, although towards the end of her reign her attitude changed slightly, and reserved the right to interfere in and try to control all his activities, but as a mother she was loving and caring. Her letters to her daughter, the Crown Princess of Prussia, contain many tributes (which incidentally demonstrate Edward's ability to charm even his critical mother): 'he is so full of good and amiable qualities . . . has a loving affectionate heart . . . I am sure no Heir Apparent was ever so nice and understanding'. The

Prince's wise decision to be on friendly terms with politicians of all parties and beliefs ruled out any fear the Queen may have entertained of her heir following the traditional pattern of attracting to himself the political opposition and forming his own party. There never was a 'Marlborough House political party'. The Marlborough House Set, or Court as it came to be called, was always a microcosm of society.

The Prince found another opportunity for social mixing in the exclusively masculine world of the London Clubs. He joined White's, one of the longest established, the Turf, the Cosmopolitan where distinguished men of all professions met for after-dinner conversation, and the Garrick, reserved for members of the theatre world. The social mix of club life accorded closely with the Prince's liberal view of Society and exactly suited his convivial temperament. He soon founded his own club, the Marlborough, in Pall Mall opposite his house. Here smoking was permitted, this being one of the Prince's habits which lasted throughout his life – he was rarely seen without a cigar – and in the bowling alley built on at the back of the club he and his friends, in their shirt-sleeves, enjoyed this popular sport.

The elegant London scene, where Alexandra's youth and beauty complemented Edward's debonair 'man-of-the-world' image, was only one facet of Edwardian Society. Under the Prince's leadership the 'country-house weekend' became an essential element in the Society programme, with his own house at Sandringham holding the centre of the stage. Edward first took Alexandra to his country house soon after their honeymoon; both loved it, the Princess especially because the countryside reminded her of Denmark. But by 1869 the house would no longer accommodate his growing family and his large house parties, and he decided to rebuild Sandringham completely. In order to be on hand to oversee the work he rented near-by Gunton Hall from his neighbour, Lord Suffield. That elegant house provided a splendid setting for entertaining, and the Prince gave a grand ball there following the New Year celebrations in 1870. Meanwhile Sandringham was being transformed. Its huge entrance door now opened directly into an impressive suite of reception rooms: the Saloon, or Hall, a large room two storeys high with a gallery at one end, the Drawing Room, much admired by Victoria as being 'very long and handsome with painted ceilings', and the Dining Room (a Ballroom, added in 1883, completed the suite). From his original house Edward retained the Conservatory, turning it into a billiard room and placing a bowling alley alongside. He landscaped the gardens, replacing a lake close to the house by two prettier ornamental ones and, displaying an unexpectedly practical grasp of estate management, installed a plant to supply gas to both house and estate. The 'Big House', as Sandringham was known locally, was all ready by the end of 1870 as the elegant setting for Edwardian 'country-house weekend' Society.

The visitor usually travelled by train to the little station of Wolferton some 2 miles from Sandringham. There he was met by a smartly turned-out carriage, with the coachman and the groom sitting up behind dressed in the Prince's livery, and driven off briskly. His luggage, usually a bulky collection of trunks, hat boxes and leather portmanteaux, and his servant or servants, were conveyed separately in more homely vehicles. The problem of what servants to take with them to Sandringham exercised many visitors who, fearful of committing social solecisms, were anxious not to take too many (thus inconveniencing their host who would have to find accommodation for them) nor unacceptable ones. When the artist Frederic Leighton, who had made Edward's acquaintance in Rome, was invited to Sandringham in 1863, he had

Edward's country house, Sandringham in Norfolk. The west front in 1864, before rebuilding work was carried out. (Royal Collection, St James's Palace. © Her Majesty The Queen)

evidently consulted his mother on this difficult point, as she confided to her daughter: 'Fred has received an invitation to Sandringham . . . if he has not found a suitable servant we are to lend him ours – Ellen's husband, a very superior person.' Every male guest, like Lord Leighton, would be expected to take at least one servant, his 'man', a valet who would unpack his clothes, press and brush them, polish his boots and shoes, help him to dress and generally be in attendance. In the same way every lady guest would take her personal maid, who would perform the same duties for her mistress as the valet would for his master, and in addition would arrange her coiffure and look after her jewellery.

The visitor, sweeping through the handsome Norfolk Gates in the Prince's carriage, would bowl up the drive to the big entrance portico, to be greeted by his host and hostess, taken into the Hall, and placed upon a special chair to be weighed. (This curious custom of weighing guests at the beginning and end of their stay and noting the results in a special book, was common at the time in big country houses and obligatory for all guests except pregnant ladies.) After tea had been served in the Hall, the visitor would be escorted to his room, probably by the Prince himself, who would see that nothing was wanting for his comfort. For first-time visitors an equerry would then slip in to explain the 'house rules' – times and arrangements for meals, whether orders should be worn, where the visitor would be seated at table, the partner he would take in on his arm and so on. Edward was an accomplished and punctilious host who planned every detail and saw to it that his whole household ran smoothly and that his guests were looked after and entertained. The Sandringham programme included walking, riding and driving round the estate. In the winter when the lakes froze, ice-skating was a popular sport; the whole household joined in, ice-hockey games were organised (Edward kept goal), the ladies, led by Alexandra who excelled in this pastime, glided around becomingly attired in furs, non-skaters were pushed about in sledges and chairs with runners; as it grew dark, lanterns lit up the scene. For after-dinner diversions tables were set up in the Drawing Room for the card players, the gentlemen played billiards and bowls; musical evenings, plays, charades, games and dancing amused the company. Sunday had a routine all to itself; the whole household attended a church service in the morning, walking across the park to the little Sandringham Church. The Prince had had a serious discussion on 'Sunday observance' with Arthur Stanley while sailing up the Nile during his tour in 1862, and wherever he happened to be, he always attended church on Sundays. (This habit of his was so well known that any omission, for instance when Edward was indisposed, provoked general and anxious comment.) After Sunday luncheon, the guests were taken on a tour of the home farm, kennels and stables. The Prince and Princess were devoted to their dogs and horses; every animal was visited, appraised and given a tit-bit. At the model dairy Alexandra presided at the tea-table, and on the way back to the Big House Edward led the company through the extensive kitchen gardens and green-houses, of which he was very proud. The Prince was an energetic and efficient landowner but Sandringham was to him, as well as to Alexandra, far more than a well-run estate. It had become a beloved home, their preferred residence to which they constantly returned, where Edward always celebrated his birthdays and spent Christmas whenever possible and to which he delighted in inviting his friends. Sunday evenings were spent in quiet amusements; not until after midnight would the Prince allow his male guests to indulge in billiards or bowls. He kept late hours, rarely getting to bed before one o'clock in the morning, but this did not prevent him from being an early riser; he was always up and dressed by eight o'clock.

The daily routine of meals played an important part in the country-house weekend. At Sandringham guests were expected to come down for breakfast between nine and ten o'clock. This was served at small tables, an innovative departure from the 'long board' and a custom which the Prince may have observed at Gunton Hall and subsequently adopted. Breakfast was a substan-tial meal; on the sideboard spirit-lamps kept hot huge silver dishes of porridge, eggs, bacon, devilled kidneys, finnan haddock, kedgeree. Another sideboard held a variety of cold meats, pressed beef, ham, tongue and game. China and Indian tea, coffee and chocolate, bread, rolls, toast, scones and muffins, jams and preserves and fresh fruit were all laid ready. Edward breakfasted alone in his rooms (as did Alexandra who was a late riser and rarely appeared before eleven o'clock). Sometimes he had only coffee and toast; at other times, and especially on shooting days, he indulged in a hearty 'cooked breakfast'. He dearly loved a bloater but believed that only one woman could prepare the slightly salted and smoked herring as he liked it, and she was the cook at Newmarket Jockey Club; only when staying there could he indulge in this favourite dish. Luncheon was taken at half-past one. At five o'clock tea was served in the Saloon; tiny sandwiches and pastries, and the Prince's favourite Scottish shortbread were handed round.

Dinner, at half-past eight, was elaborate and elegant; the long table was covered with snowy linen, sparkling crystal, silver dishes and flowers; while the guests ate, a band played. The number of courses served varied with the occasion. For a large State Dinner, or when important visitors were present, a typical menu, always written in French, might be: *Potages* (Soups), two kinds, one clear with assorted garnishes, and the other thick or creamy; *Poissons* (Fish) a choice of fried fish – small fillets or small whole fish such as whitebait – and a poached fish such as turbot with a wine sauce; then the *Entrée*, an intermediate course between fish and meat, usually consisting of dishes prepared with poultry or duck sometimes in pastry, such as vol-au-vent, a puff pastry case with creamy chicken filling, or foie gras in a pastry cover. This was followed by the *Relevé* (the Remove) which today would be called the main course or roast, consisting of roast or braised meat often served with a spicy sauce to which wine and brandy had been added; the next course, the oddly named *Rot* (Roast) consisted of game birds in season – pheasant, partridge, woodcock, quail and grouse. The last course to be named on the menu, the *Entremets*, was a strange mixture of dishes, a typical selection being: asparagus served warm with a *sauce mousseline* (a Hollandaise sauce lightened with stiffly beaten egg-whites), reputedly one of Edward's favourite dishes; a hot baked pudding such as Apple Charlotte; a cold sweet such as *Rod Grod*, Alexandra's favourite Danish confection (the juice of cooked redcurrants and raspberries was sweetened, thickened with cornflour, chilled in little basins and served with cream); and a savoury such as *Croutes au jambon* (creamed chopped ham on tiny circles of fried bread). The Dessert did not figure on the written menu; it always consisted of fresh fruit, glacé or crystallised fruit, ices, chocolates, bon-bons and little sweet biscuits. A side-table in the Dining Room was always set during dinner with a selection of hot and cold fowls, hot and cold roast beef and tongue, from which guests could ask to be served. Today's diner will notice the absence of vegetables and of a cheese-board. Plainly cooked vegetables sometimes accompanied the Remove, but were far more likely to be found among the *Entremets*, not served plain but 'dressed' in a variety of ways, perhaps tiny peas cooked with mint and lettuce and tossed in butter, or sprigs of cauliflower coated with white sauce or browned breadcrumbs. As for cheese, this was never served as a separate course as is today's custom; the reason may have been that soft foreign cheeses could not be transported while chunks of home-produced cheese were possibly considered as lacking refinement and certainly as not showing off the art of the chefs. These culinary experts, however, used cheese extensively in the preparation of their masterpieces. Wine was served throughout dinner, but in a hard-drinking age the Prince was moderate in habit, usually drinking only a couple of glasses of his favourite champagne.

The composition of such an elaborate menu required a great deal of careful planning, since the dishes had to be pleasing not only to the palate but also to the eye. The *Entrée* formed a kind of artistic centrepiece to the meal; daintiness and preparation were all-important for these concoctions which were presented on their serving dishes by footmen and came under close scrutiny; no effort was spared by the chef to produce attractive effects. The preparation required for one of Alexandra's favourite *entrées*, *Poulet Danois* (Chicken Danish-style) is an apt illustration: a large chicken was stuffed with butter, lemon juice and chopped parsley, put in a casserole with carrot, onion and bayleaf and cooked in a slow oven for an hour and a half; it had to be carefully watched so that it remained white. A sauce was then made with the chicken juices, stock and cream. Home-made noodles sauted in butter were arranged on a large serving dish, the chicken, cut up in pieces, laid on top and the whole covered with the creamy sauce. As a final touch, before the piping-hot dish was rushed from the kitchen to the Dining Room, it was garnished with tiny pieces of red tongue, thus adding some colour to an otherwise pure-white appearance and delicately indicating Denmark's national colours of red and white. Other dishes were even more laborious to prepare: poached salmon trout were skinned, all the bones removed, the flesh put together again, the head and tail laid in position and the reconstituted fish glazed with claret jelly. This glazing had to be done by degrees and several applications were usually needed to get a good coating. This pretty pink dish, tastefully garnished, was one of Edward's favourites for luncheon parties and it also appeared at his opera suppers. For these elegant affairs footmen took the cloths, plates, silver and glasses to a private room in the opera house in the afternoon and set out the tables. The food followed later in hampers. A typical menu would include cold consommé, lobster mayonnaise, the pink jellied trout, duck, lamb cutlets, plovers' eggs, chicken, tongue and ham galantine, assorted little sandwiches, fruit desserts and pastries.

Edward certainly liked French cooking, but he also appreciated English fare and introduced a custom which was extremely popular with his household; this was to serve on Sunday evenings a simple dinner of roast beef, with plain roasted potatoes, horseradish sauce and Yorkshire pudding. And for the Sandringham shooting parties, important social occasions, the luncheon menus consisted almost entirely of similarly homely fare – Scotch broth, Mulligatawny soup, hashed venison, stewed mutton, Irish stew and game pies satisfied the shooters' hearty appetites and the meal was often rounded off by a plum or Christmas pudding, a favourite of the Prince. How was all this food kept hot and conveyed, often for considerable distances over rough fields, to the marquee erected near the line of guns? Edward, whose attention to detail often surprises, had solved this problem with his 'Hot-Box'. This was a large padded box with deep recesses into which heavy containers with close-fitting lids fitted snugly. The food was cooked early in the morning, put into the containers and the heavy padded lid shut down, remaining tightly closed until required when the food was brought out, piping hot and appetising. The Prince's Hot-Box was used on many occasions; as well as for shooting parties, it served for picnic lunches, for meals on train journeys and later for motor car outings. (It also made a reappearance during the First World War when, fitted on the back of a lorry, it visited the front line with Edward's son, King George V.)

Shooting was one of the Prince's passions. Taught to handle a gun before he was thirteen, he shot regularly over the Windsor coverts; on visits to Balmoral he was instructed in deer stalking. Travelling round the world as a young man, he pursued this passion whenever possible, bagging wild boar in Albania, prairie fowl in America and returning with a mixed bag of trophies from the Middle East. Once settled at Sandringham, where game was plentiful and conditions particularly suitable for rearing pheasant and partridge, he directed his energies towards building up a large and successful 'shoot'. Edward's first gun was a single-barrel muzzle-loading percussion type. By the time the Sandringham shoots were in full swing, the breech-loading gun had come into fashion. This facilitated shooting, since loading was much quicker and easier. Like most huntsmen Edward used dogs to flush out the game, but for big shoots he also employed beaters, usually farm labourers from his estate, whose job was to drive the birds into the air towards the guns. Big shoots at Sandringham were exciting occasions and the day started early. Like his neighbour Lord Leicester at Holkham Hall, the Prince kept all his Sandring-ham clocks set half-an-hour in advance; a shoot scheduled to start at 'ten o'clock Sandringham time' would actually be starting at 'half-past nine real time'. This daylight-saving device was used to get as much sport into the day as possible (in Edward's case it may also have been a – vain – attempt to cure Alexandra's incorrigible unpunctuality).

The Sandringham gamekeepers, smartly turned-out in green velveteen coats, placed the shooters, each with his loader kneeling behind, in a line, and set the beaters in action. The birds came over in swarms, the guns cracked out in a rattling fusillade, the bag was collected up by the well-trained dogs and the shooters moved on to the next line. By midday everyone was ready for lunch and made their way to the marquee where straw had been strewn on the

A Big Shoot at Sandringham in 1867, by Thomas Jones Barker.
(Royal Collection, St James's Palace. © Her Majesty The Queen)

ground, long wooden tables set up and the Hot Box was waiting. At this moment the ladies joined the party, having walked across the fields or been driven there in carriages from the Big House. The morning bag was laid out beside the marquee and the Prince read out the numbers of birds accredited to each gun, to general applause or mock disapproval. In this convivial atmosphere the party then partook of the excellent contents of the Hot Box. Shooting continued during the afternoon until the light went, and the ladies remained to watch, each sitting on a camp stool behind a shooter and talking to him between volleys. Edward, while delighting in female company, did not approve of feminine participation in sports and no lady, anxious to retain her place in Society, would have dared to offend her host by trying to adopt a more active role.

Edwardian Society, as created by the Prince, in fact teemed with unwritten laws, conventions and behavioural patterns, a veritable jungle for the unwary and the aspirant trying to get 'in'. An area which assumed increasing importance was that of dress, and this was particularly so for ladies. Their role, on the whole, was confined to being decorative and for this a very extensive wardrobe was required. By the time the ladies joined the gentlemen at the shoot, they would already have arrived at their second change of clothes, having discarded their neat morning dress for voluminous tweed skirts, fur jackets and capes, huge hats, buttoned boots and the correct accessories of fur muffs, gloves and walking sticks. On returning to the Big House for tea, the ladies changed quickly into their tea gowns; these were lovely creations of silk and satin, draped with frilled and pleated chiffon, spangled with gold, banded with white fur, adorned with huge fluttery angel sleeves. Reclining round the tea-table in these sumptuous confections the ladies listened to stories of the shoot and then retired to their rooms for the most important event of the day, getting dressed for dinner.

Alexandra dressed for sailing on the royal yacht *Osborne* in 1880.
(National Portrait Gallery, London; photograph by Symonds and Co.)

Current fashion and taste decreed that all ladies, whatever their figure, must achieve the 'hourglass silhouette' – a low, prominent and over-hanging bust, tiny waist, swelling hips – a model popularised by the famous artist, Charles Dana Gibson, and nicknamed 'the Gibson Girl'. All Society women and famous beauties had to conform to this fashionable look. To attain it, corsets, or stays, were indispensable. These formidable garments were laced in tightly to reduce the waist to some 25 to 21 inches (some courageous ladies managed 19); they were so long and stiff that walking became difficult. Ladies cultivated a gliding step, appearing to swim across the floor. The lady's maid, having got her mistress into her corset, chemise and petticoat, arranged her coiffure. The evening dress was then put on; this was usually of silk or satin, often white, low cut with frills and draperies over the bust, puffed sleeves, very tightly fitting over the hips to give the required svelte line and with the material pulled round to the back to give a 'bustle' effect. Long white gloves, an ornate fan, a posy of flowers in a pretty holder and, an essential item, jewellery completed the ensemble.

Alexandra, who had first entered the social scene in her girlish crinolines, loose ringlets to her shoulders and modest trinkets, soon became the leader of fashion. Always slim, in fact thin, the close-fitting 'Princess' line suited her to perfection. Her jewellery box filled up rapidly with wedding presents, her husband delighted in buying her attractive pieces (this provoked 'jobations' from Victoria) and from his tour in 1875 brought her home a treasure-chest of Indian jewels. From this accumulated hoard the Princess devised four types of jewelled adornments which will always be associated with her and which became all the rage for Edwardian ladies. These were the choker, a wide necklace of three, four or sometimes more strands of jewels, usually pearls, worn high and tight round the neck; the *sautoir* (an echo of sixteenth-century fashion), a very long rope of pearls arranged to hang in several loops to well below the waist (wearing the dangling *sautoir* was not without its hazards: Alexandra once caught hers in the carriage-door on her way to the State Opening of Parliament, scattering pearls everywhere and holding up the ceremony); the medievally inspired stomacher, a low-slung waist-belt heavily swagged with jewels; and the aigrette, a small head ornament of a feathered crest attached to a jewelled band or clasp placed on a piled-up coiffure. Alexandra's innovations were rapidly copied and jewellery became an essential item in the wardrobe of every Society lady.

But not every newcomer could compete in this respect. When Mrs Lillie Langtry, who was to join the ranks of Edward's 'lady friends' and form an intimate relationship with him, came to London, her wardrobe, as she herself described it, consisted of one simple black dress, made up for her by a dressmaker at her home in Jersey. In this dress, wearing no jewels, since she had none, and with her hair twisted into a knot at the nape of her neck, the 'Jersey Lily' took London by storm; her success owed nothing to dress but everything to her beauty. After her first party, she described her amazement as the invitations poured in and the black dress had to do duty evening after evening. By the time Mrs Langtry had been painted by every fashionable artist and had been introduced to the Prince, she was able to discard the somewhat battered black dress and extend her wardrobe, acquiring, for example, what she called a classically severe gown of white velvet embroidered with pearls. Her acceptance 'into' Society, under Edward's patronage, was signified by her presentation at Court. This occurred at one of Victoria's afternoon 'Drawing Rooms'. Mrs Langtry's gown was of ivory brocade, garlanded with pale yellow roses; her Court train hanging from her shoulders was of the same material lined with yellow silk. Her bouquet of yellow roses had been obligingly chosen by the Prince as an exact match. Getting dressed took Mrs Langtry, assisted by her mother and aunt, all morning. Then, thrilling with excitement and emotion, she lined up with the other ladies to make her curtsey to the Queen (who was apparently very eager to see the famous beauty). Startled to hear the Lord Chamberlain's whisper of 'Mrs Langtry comes next, Your Majesty', she nevertheless managed to make a perfect curtsey, kiss the Queen's hand and repeat this obeisance to the Prince and Princess of Wales and other royalties standing in line. Then came the most difficult part of the performance, feared by all the ladies at the Presentation Ceremony and to fail at which would be a social blunder in the highest degree, namely how to exit in a dignified manner, walking backwards and encumbered by a long, heavy train hanging from one's shoulders. This manoeuvre required the assistance of a page; bundling up the mass of material he threw it to the lady who had to catch it on her left arm – her right being fully occupied with fan and bouquet – and then retreat gracefully. Mrs Langtry and her page accomplished this complicated finale, and her final social accolade came with an invitation to a ball at Marlborough House that same evening.

Edward's interest in fashion was not confined to buying dresses and jewels for Alexandra; he had always shown an interest in his own clothes. His early efforts to create his individual style had provoked gloomy accusations of 'dandyism' from his father and irritable remarks from his mother about his 'loose long jackets'. But none of this deterred the Prince. Once launched in his Society he became a natural trend-setter. Everything he did, and especially everything he wore, was closely scrutinised and copied. His contributions to what the smart man was wearing included clothes for country pursuits, the

Edward wearing the Homburg hat, Inverness coat, spats and elegant walking-cane which he popularised, and holding his inevitable cigar, *c.*1896.
(National Portrait Gallery, London; photograph by Hills and Saunders)

comfortable single-breasted, waist-belted Norfolk tweed jacket, worn with knee-breeches, thick knitted stockings and gaiters, and the Homburg hat worn, as Edward wore all his hats, slightly tilted to one side. He revived the popularity of the long tweed Inverness coat with shoulder-capes. And on the long hot journey to India when social convention demanded that his all-male suite appear for dinner in full dress, he substituted for the heavy 'tails' a short lightweight jacket with silk facings which became the standard dinner jacket. The prince was a neat and meticulous dresser and imposed these habits on Society. Slovenly apparel was never permitted; shirt-sleeves were allowed in the bowling alley but nowhere else. He had a quick eye for lapses such as a white tie worn instead of black, clothes unsuitable for the occasion, orders incorrectly displayed on the coat lapel, but in this respect, when the situation demanded, he could be a master of consideration for other people's feelings. In 1884 he invited to Sandringham for the weekend a working-class MP, Mr Henry Broadhurst, with whom he had sat on a Commission. Knowing that Mr Broadhurst had no evening clothes he arranged informal dinners with the result that his gratified guest departed after a successful visit feeling, as he put it, that he had spent the weekend with an old chum from his own background. Edward liked wearing uniforms, having always hankered after a military career, and many of his public appearances, including his wedding, were made in this garb. But the image by which he was best known, and will always be remembered, was that of the debonair man-about-town. Whether in his smart black jacket, light-coloured or checked trousers, grey spats, shapely boots, black silky top hat at a rakish angle, gloves and cane and the inevitable cigar, or in his immaculate evening clothes with gleaming stiff shirt and a flower in his buttonhole, he became a popular model. Men of all classes wanted to look like the Prince, to 'cut a dash', to be 'a bit of a lad', to swagger about with a cane. In a somewhat bizarre role reversal these aspirations were personified on the music hall stages of the time by the enormously popular

Edward as a 'man-about-
town', c.1875.
(Camera Press, London;
photograph by Bassano, G56)

'male impersonators' like Vesta Tilley who, swaggering about in smart evening dress, regularly brought the house down with her song 'Burlington Bertie'.

How had it come about that Edward's image was so well known, not only intimately to his immediate set, but widely to the general public? The answer lies partly in the technical improvements to the camera and the increasing popularity of photographs. Edward and photography came into the world almost simultaneously, and he grew up accustomed to being photographed on every conceivable occasion. By the time his marriage was being arranged the photograph had to some extent replaced the painted portrait and taken over some of its functions. It was through the medium of photography that the Prince inspected his prospective brides. And by the time Alexandra reached London for her wedding the whole country, flooded with photographs of this beautiful girl, was well acquainted with its future Princess. Photographic studies – the modern studio portrait – in which the sitter was posed as if for a painted picture, became immensely popular. Edward called this new art form a 'photo-portrait' when he admired one taken of his artist friend Frederic Leighton and asked for a copy. Sitters sometimes posed in fancy-dress – the painter Millais had himself photographed in costume as Dante – or were arranged in groups which 'told a story' in the manner of popular paintings of the time. A royal example of this trend was the photograph taken after the Prince's wedding ceremony; members of the royal family, including in-laws, are grouped solemnly around the bust of Albert, and as if to duplicate the illusion that her dead husband is present, Victoria holds his framed portrait and shows it to the kneeling children (only the Prince, and his Princess

Sir John Everett Millais (1829–1896),
photographed in costume as Dante, by
David Wilkie Wynfield in the 1860s.
(National Portrait Gallery, London)

clinging to her new husband, appear to be oblivious of the 'story' element and gaze straight at the camera). Since numerous copies of the 'photo-portrait' could be obtained from one plate, collecting them became a craze. Everybody wanted to have these postcard-size pictures of royalty and people 'in the news'. This included the Society beauties whose lovely faces gazed soulfully from shop windows. Among these ladies was Mrs Langtry. Although she appeared in many painted pictures, it was through her photographs that her astonishing beauty became known to the public, so well-known indeed that crowds rushed to Hyde Park when she was riding or driving there and stood on the park chairs to watch her go by.

The camera, as well as producing portraits, was beginning to develop another function, that of the documentary. Victoria sent the photographer Roger Fenton out to Balaclava in 1855 to take some 400 photographs in the Crimea. Fenton has been called 'the first war photographer', although his pictures were all taken after the event and consist mainly of scenes associated with the Crimean War, posed groups of participants and so on; nevertheless they vividly document the glories and miseries of war. (In the 1860s the Civil War in the United States was similarly documented in photographs). And in 1856 the intrepid photographer Francis Frith, roaming the Middle East on the backs of dromedaries, 'shot' the Biblical scenery which Edward visited a few years later. Edwardian Society quickly adapted itself to both the photo-portrait and the documentary element of the camera. Almost every country-house party ended with a group photograph of the guests. Many of the strained expressions in such photographs must have been due to the wearisomely long periods of immobility required. In sending some to a friend the Prince commented that 'they might have been better – of course, the ladies moved!'. (Edward's interest in photography never waned. As King he tightened up control, which in Victoria's time had become very lax, of photography in the royal palaces, by allowing access only to accredited photographers and assuming copyright of every photograph.)

Through the eye of the camera Edwardian Society appears as a study in black and white; this impression is reinforced when photographs are laid

Mrs Lillie Langtry, photographed in 1885 in the Van der Weyde studios (the first to use artificial lighting) during her stage career, playing the leading role of Lady Ormond in *Peril*, an adaptation of Victorien Sardou's 1861 success, *Nos Intimes*. Her large feathered fan recalls the Prince of Wales' feathered crest.
(National Portrait Gallery, London)

beside examples of contemporary art – the profusion of pen-and-ink satirical caricatures, Charles Dana Gibson's pen drawings of his voluptuous ladies, Aubrey Beardsley's black-and-white gallery of exotics, the sketches in the illustrated papers. And an Edwardian may well have felt that these black-and-white images faithfully reflected the world in which he moved. Men's clothes were usually dark-coloured, often black, shirts a gleaming white, as was the flower in their buttonhole (Oscar Wilde joked at this convention with his 'green carnation'). Ladies often wore white dresses, which were compulsory for Court appearances and the recognised party attire for young girls. In any case fashion-conscious ladies had realised that white, or black, dresses provided the most effective background to show off their glittering jewellery. One of the most successful outfits of the Princess, who had first captivated Victoria in a simple black dress, was an evening dress and train of black satin, trimmed only with sprays of white lilac, but among which gleamed and sparkled her fabulous swags, loops, *sautoirs* and brooches of pearls and diamonds. To our colour-saturated eyes, Edwardian Society's black-and-white image might appear stark, but undeniably elegant and sophisticated.

The stylish leader of this Society imposed upon it a complicated set of conventions, but Edward's own personal code of conduct was simple and straightforward. Writing to a friend he declared firmly: 'I may and have many faults – no one is more alive to them than I am; but I have held one great principle in life from which I will never waver, and that is loyalty to one's friends and defending them if possible when they get into trouble. One often gets into scrapes in consequence but I consider the risk worth running.' The

Photography methods in 1875. The professional photographer has hung a light curtain behind his sitters and has posed the two men, Edward and his brother-in-law the King of Greece, symmetrically at each side of the lady, the Queen of Greece, and stands ready beside his huge camera-stand with a large photographic plate in his hand.
(The *Illustrated London News* Picture Library)

Prince certainly did get into 'scrapes' as he called them, which at the time annoyed Victoria, worried her Ministers, diverted the public and which, in after years, provoked many moralising comments. But these judgements have become somewhat modified with the realisation that it is in fact quite surprising that a young man, denied proper employment, excluded from his mother's confidence yet, because of her refusal to perform the usual public duties of a monarch, forced into the limelight and, by reason of his position as heir-in-waiting, always in the glare of publicity, did not get into more 'scrapes'. And this is all the more so when Edward's character and temperament are taken into account. His nature was social and convivial. Smiling, nonchalant, dapper, elegant and sophisticated, easy in any company – and in this respect the very opposite of his father and mother – he would always have been, in any rank of life, the popular centre of a crowd.

To his social inclinations, to the strict conventions of the Society he had brought into being and to his absolute loyalty to his friends, may be attributed some of his much-publicised 'scrapes'. These included having to appear as a witness in 1870 in the Mordaunt divorce case in which two of his friends were cited as co-respondents, and where the revelation that he had written letters, albeit very trivial ones, to Lady Mordaunt aroused much public interest and speculation. Backed up by his mother and wife, the Prince emerged unscathed but with his popularity temporarily diminished. He suffered the tribulations and enjoyed the successes of any figure in the public eye. His popularity fluctuated, sometimes reaching extraordinary heights as after his near-fatal illness in 1871, sometimes plummeting to the depths as after the 'baccarat scandal' in 1891. The Prince had been a house-party guest at Tranby Croft during Doncaster Race Week in September 1890. On two consecutive evenings when the card game of baccarat was played, one of the guests, a serving army officer, was seen by several of the players to cheat, and win. Edward, who held the bank, noticed nothing. Cheating at cards was considered one of the most reprehensible acts in a Society which held that the honour of a gentleman, and officer, must be inviolate. To avoid scandal the accused man was asked to sign a paper to the effect that he would never play cards again, on the understanding that the affair would be kept secret. All the guests, including the Prince, later signed this paper. But the secret got out, the officer brought a case against his original accusers and Edward found himself implicated. 'This horrible Trial', as he called it, dragged on until June 1891, when the jury brought in a verdict against the officer. But the fate of this unhappy man, who faced dismissal from the army and social ostracism, was by this time of no interest to the general public, for whom it was the Prince himself who was, as it were, on trial for his way of life. Although his action had been motivated by loyalty to his friends, and although he was again supported by the Queen – whose only reproach was that he should not have signed the paper – and Alexandra, the Prince found himself castigated by the press for his gambling activities. Baccarat was labelled 'illegal', the revelation that the Prince had a personal set of counters for the game engraved with his crest provoked volleys of criticism and leading churchmen urged him to mend his ways. Edward substituted bridge for baccarat and quietly rode out this storm, but another was about to break over his head, for the somewhat bizarre reason that one of his close friends, naval officer Lord Charles Beresford, had committed adultery. Lord Charles had an affair with a beautiful young married woman, Lady Brooke. When he returned to sea, Lady Brooke discovered that Lord Charles's wife, a lady of impeccable morals, was pregnant, whereupon she wrote a furious letter to her lover accusing him of 'infidelity' to her with his own wife. By an unlucky chance this letter did not reach Lord Charles but fell into the hands of Lady Beresford who immediately took steps to denounce Lady Brooke. Into this ridiculous situation, with a scenario worthy of a theatrical farce, came the Prince, dragged in by Lady Brooke who begged him to save her from social ostracism. Edward promptly fell for this 'beauty in distress'. His entreaties to Lady Beresford to return the letter falling on deaf ears, he removed her name from his invitation list, this being the equivalent of social death. Angry scenes, talk of duels, writing of pamphlets 'revealing all' and threats of unpleasant publicity for the Prince followed in quick succession. Not until the Prime Minister of the day, Lord Salisbury, had been called in did the dust settle. The consequences of what was in essence a personal, and fairly trivial affair, were however twofold and far-reaching. Edward never really forgave Beresford, and in the row over navy reform which broke out during his reign between Beresford and First Lord of the Admiralty John Fisher, he supported the latter. And the Prince's susceptibility to pretty women – long since recognised in his own set – had now, by his friendship with Lady Brooke, become common knowledge.

Edwardian Society flourished in an age of arranged marriages, unions contrived by parents, or their legal advisers, to join estates or to provide funds in the form of dowries and settlements. Edward's own marriage was of this type, arranged by his father not for financial, but for political and dynastic reasons. Edward and Alexandra expressed an inclination for each other, but many arranged marriages were loveless, and in these circumstances Society was inclined to condone extramarital affairs, so long as they were discreet. (Lady Brooke's liaison with Beresford would have gone unremarked had she not over-ridden conventions with her imprudent letter.) Edward delighted in feminine company and enjoyed being surrounded by the beautiful, voluptuous women of his set. His name was romantically linked with many attractive ladies (although it is worthy of note that he never allowed any of these companions to exert the slightest political pressure upon him.) His special favourite was Mrs Alice Keppel, daughter of Admiral Sir William Edmonstone, and wife of George Keppel, a younger son of the Earl of

Mrs Alice Keppel.
Lithograph by F Jenkins
after Ellis Roberts.
(National Portrait Gallery,
London)

Mrs Alice Keppel with her husband George and daughter
Violet, c.1907.
(The Hulton Picture Company)

Albemarle. The Prince first met Mrs Keppel, then aged twenty-nine, in February 1898 at a dinner party. Almost overnight there developed between them a friendship, and companionship, which was to last until his death. This beautiful and stately woman, as kind and loyal as she was charming, was also witty and entertaining, as the following incident, which took place after Edward became King, illustrates. During a game of bridge in which they were partners, Edward, as dummy, put down a terrible hand of cards on which he had pushed up his partner. Mrs Keppel, who had to play the hand with her equally bad one, took one look at the cards and exclaimed: 'All I can say, Sire, is God Save the King and preserve Mrs Keppel!' Mrs Keppel and her tall, handsome husband became regular guests at Sandringham and at the country houses visited by Edward and Alexandra.

The Prince had perfected the 'country-house weekend' at Sandringham; and members of his set vied with each other to invite him to their houses for similar entertainments. This practice became a regular feature of Edwardian Society life and a permanent element in that of Edward both as Prince and King. In the early days of such 'royal visitations' many inexperienced hosts became panicky about the complicated arrangements to be made. Rooms were quickly re-decorated, new curtains hung, all the best pieces of furniture moved into the royal suite, masses of flowers arranged everywhere. Other considerations worried the Duke of Devonshire when he was expecting the royal couple at Chatsworth in 1872. His son, fortuitously staying at Sandringham, was bombarded with anxious questions. Could he find out how many servants the Prince would bring? How many maids for the Princess? Would he bring his own horses since the Duke was afraid the Chatsworth ones would bolt at the noise of cheering? But as the century wore on and after 'The Prince' became 'The King', such arrangements had become routine. Hosts dealt efficiently with setting up a 'telegraph room' for urgent messages, with the

King Edward and members of a country-house party at West Dean Park, Chichester,
23 November 1904. Alice and George Keppel stand in the back row, Mrs Keppel directly
behind Edward.
(National Portrait Gallery, London; photograph by J Russell and Sons)

mountains of luggage sent on ahead of the royal guests in two huge wagons
known as 'foregones' and with the crowd of equerries, secretaries and servants
including maids, valets, footmen, loaders for shooting days and grooms.

The style, glamour and elegance of Edwardian Society was underpinned by
a veritable army of servants, many of them working away invisibly below-
stairs, others always on duty in their smart uniforms. What were their lives
like and how were they treated by their masters? Reminiscences have revealed
that life in the servants' hall had as many ups-and-downs and as strict a
hierarchical system as Society itself. As for their treatment, here again the
Prince was a trend-setter. From an early age he adopted the habit of using the
same courteous manners to all. Practical and with a keen eye to detail, he
demanded efficiency from his staff; but all services were acknowledged with a
word of thanks and a charming smile. Lady Fildes, wife of the artist Sir Luke
Fildes, noticed that when Edward, as King, visited her husband for a portrait
sitting, he bowed and smiled to her maid Mary when he passed her in the hall
(Mary of course was very excited). At Sandringham Christmas festivities the
Tree held a present for every member of the staff, and Edward danced
indefatigably until the small hours at the annual Servants Ball. 'He is so kind to
all below him, for which he is universally loved', observed his mother.

Innovative in his behaviour to servants, and innovative in admitting to his
circle members of all classes and professions, the Prince introduced yet
another element to the lifestyle of Edwardian Society. His visits to the
Continent were soon copied and to congregate in the South of France or to
'take the waters' at some spa became fashionable pursuits. Social insularity
began to yield to cosmopolitanism.

6

PRINCELY DUTIES, PRINCELY PLEASURES

*A*FTER HIS marriage, and during the forty years of his 'in waiting' for the throne, Edward combined his interest in 'foreign relations' with his position as creator of Edwardian Society. But there was yet another side to the Prince's life – and perhaps it was the one in which he excelled – where he made, and perfected, a new role for the monarchy, that of public appearances. As a young unmarried Queen, Victoria had performed various public duties, although, as she herself admitted, her shyness and nervousness made such occasions a painful effort. When her husband became Prince Consort, he undertook many social functions on her behalf. After his death, in her inconsolable widowhood she withdrew even more, fleeing from what she considered the morbid curiosity of the public. The retreat of the Court from London caused the social vacuum which Edward had to fill. He also found himself called upon to take the place of his mother in representing the Crown.

When Albert carefully planned the training of his son, he regarded the foreign tours on which he sent him as educational opportunities. But he had completely misunderstood the boy's character. In Rome, Edward dutifully visited and described the antiquities, but his real interest was not in these, nor in the books he was supposed to be reading, but in the people he met. The Prince's temperament responded to an audience; he soon taught himself how to rise to any occasion and deal with the unexpected. During his successful tours in the New World everyone noticed that he never showed impatience or resentment when things did not go according to plan. When the ballroom floor collapsed in New York Edward, quite unabashed by this misadventure and the enormous crush of people, strolled about, chatting pleasantly, until the dancing could begin. This sang-froid never left him throughout his public life, and it was increased by his own efforts. On his accession to the throne in 1901 he appointed Sir Lionel Cust, Director of the National Portrait Gallery, to be Surveyor of the King's Pictures and to hold a post at Court. Sir Lionel, who was thus with the King on many public occasions, perceptively noted that he had trained himself, like an actor, in expression and deportment, and to execute entrances and exits with decorum and dignity. To these technical accomplishments he added his habits of punctuality and attention to detail. But the Prince possessed another quality which has often been remarked upon, namely his kindness to those whom he met in public life and his ability to put them at their ease. A perspiring and tongue-tied official would receive a beaming smile and a jovial word to get him started. Upon one occasion, a stage whisper of 'Hand it to me!' to a nervous Councillor who had lost his head and thrown his Address of Welcome into the waste-paper basket, retrieved an awkward situation, with Edward somehow contriving to make it appear that this was correct procedure.

Whether it is true that the Prince never read books is a moot point – he certainly adopted the politician's, and diplomat's, custom of going through the newspapers every day, and in his case this included the French and German ones – but he did read people, filing away their names and faces in his memory and retaining even the smallest details about them. The artist Holman Hunt noticed this 'extraordinary faculty', as he called it, as early as 1863, when Edward came to look at his painting, *London Bridge by Night on the occasion of the Prince's marriage.* He recorded:

> Suddenly singling out Mr Combe's figure which I had introduced into
> the crowd with face no larger than a sixpence, the Prince exclaimed: 'I
> know that man! Wait a minute,' he added, 'I have seen him in the
> hunting-field with Lord Macclesfield's hounds. He rides a clever pony
> about fourteen hands high, and his beard blows over his shoulders. He
> is the head of a house of Oxford and not a College' – as he went on
> following the trace in his mind – 'but I'll tell you – Yes – I remember now
> – it's the Printing Press and he rides in a red jacket. Am I right?' 'Your
> Royal Highness is surprisingly so,' I answered. 'Remind me of his name,'
> said the Prince. Before I had well said it he took me up with 'Yes, I
> remember, Combe, of course.'

This graphic account exemplifies Edward's already well-developed memory
for faces and their visual associations.

How did the Prince acquire that vital requisite for any successful public
figure, the ability to deliver, or 'put over' a speech? On his New World tour his
clear diction, when reading statements prepared by his Governor and advisers, had been highly commended. His first attempt to speak 'off his own bat',
as it were, came soon after his marriage, when he was called upon to reply to
the toast to his health at the annual banquet of the Royal Academy of Arts in
May 1863. Edward prepared a short speech of thanks, mentioning his father's
interest in the Academy and his own pleasure at the enthusiasm aroused by
his marriage and so on. He carefully learned it by heart. On the morning of the
dinner he was word-perfect, in the middle of the speech he 'dried up'; while
the rather embarrassed audience waited he went through it in his mind,
recovered the thread and finished it to relieved applause. After this experience
he decided never again to try to learn a speech by heart, but evolved his own
method. This consisted of jotting down only a few words as headings to
remind him of key points; from these he improvised his discourse. A year
later, called upon to act as Chairman of the Royal Literary Fund dinner, a large
affair with some 500 guests at which he would have to give several speeches,
he tried out his new system. This was deemed a resounding success by the
critical auditors, one of whom reported that he did not even have to glance at
his few notes. Writing to Mrs Bruce, widow of his old Governor, the Prince
modestly described his evening: 'Many thanks for your congratulations on my
first attempt as Chairman of a public dinner. It is a very good thing over, as I
was very nervous at first, but felt more at home after the first two speeches.'
Thereafter he employed his chosen style, developing into an accomplished
and fluent speaker and equally at home improvising in French and German as
well.

His public engagements multiplied. In 1871 he wrote to his mother:

> You have no conception of the quantity of applications we get, in the
> course of the year, to open this place, lay a stone, attend public dinners,
> luncheons, fetes without end; and sometimes people will not take no for
> an answer. I certainly think we must be made of wood or iron if we could
> go through all they ask, and all these things have increased tenfold since
> the last ten years.

Two years earlier the Prince, who had no desire to usurp his mother's position
in public duties, had gently urged her to make an occasional appearance,

pointing out that everyone, not only Londoners, hated to see Buckingham Palace unoccupied. To Victoria's defensive argument that her nerves could not stand the noise in the capital, he replied persuasively: 'If you sometimes even came to London from Windsor – say for luncheon – and then drive for an hour in the park (where there is no noise) and then returned to Windsor, the people would be overjoyed – beyond measure', adding a rider which emphasises his preoccupation with the political situation: 'We live in radical times, and the more the people see the Sovereign the better it is for the people and the country.' Edward's advice was ignored, as was a similar observation of his that the Queen's absence from London made it more necessary that he and Alexandra should do all they could for 'trade and public matters'.

Trade was indeed assuming great importance in a rapidly industrialising Britain. Albert's Great Exhibition of 1851 had given it an enormous boost. 'Manufactories' (factories) were springing up all over the provinces, and a new class of men, the rich and successful factory owners, were entering Parliament and aspiring to enter Society. Arthur Stanley, the Prince's guide on his Middle East tour in 1862, when recalling his young charge's willingness to listen politely to long archaeological explanations in which he had scant interest, confessed how 'vexed and tired' he himself would be if he were 'dragged about to see manufactories and hear explanations of making' (production processes). Stanley was unwittingly prophetic in that such visits were destined to occupy a large part of the heir's public duties as the century wore on. Edward, however, more in touch with social changes than his mother, was alive to the importance of encouraging 'manufactories' and their owners and submitted readily and cheerfully to all such 'dragging-about', generally

Edward's visit to Tyneside in 1884. The royal procession passing along Grey Street, Newcastle-upon-Tyne. The tradespeople in the street clubbed together to erect the huge Triumphal Arch, with its proud motto: 'Semper fidelis'. (Newcastle upon Tyne City Libraries and Arts)

managing to make his gratified audiences feel that it was the very thing he most desired to do.

In 1874 the Prince arranged to visit three factories in Birmingham. This was an industrial visit with political overtones. Radicalism had diminished sharply after Edward's recovery from his near-fatal illness, but Birmingham had remained something of a Radical stronghold under the leadership of Joseph Chamberlain. Son of a screw manufacturer, Chamberlain studied in London and then went into trade in Birmingham, becoming Mayor of that city in 1873. His political views were radical and republican. How would the Prince be received by a Mayor with such leanings? Everyone expected awkwardness, unpleasantness or worse. But the visit passed off well. Driving through crowded, gaily decorated and be-flagged streets in a big procession with the Mayor and his reception committee and a military escort, the royal visitors received an Address of Welcome at the Town Hall and lunched at the headquarters of the Royal Society of Artists. At this function Chamberlain discreetly phrased the toast to his guest: 'Here in England the throne is recognised and respected as the symbol of all constitutional authority and settled government.' The future King, urbane and charming as usual, was equally tactful and ambiguous. In the afternoon visits were made to a silver and electro-plate works, a factory producing steel-pens and the premises of medal and coin makers, and the visitors were escorted all the way back to the borough boundary. Edward's bold foray into the Radical camp had interesting results. Chamberlain became MP for Birmingham in 1876; his early beliefs gradually veered towards Liberalism-Conservatism and within five years of the visit he was being entertained at Marlborough House and admitted into the Prince's social circle.

As Edward had observed to his mother, his public duties were increasing. Towns vied with each other to get him to come when they realised the publicity value of his presence. Applications were sometimes made years in advance, as happened for his visit to Tyneside in 1884. The Tyne Improvement Commissioners were determined to get the Prince to open their New Dock at North Shields and put in their request in 1882. When he eventually agreed, the Mayor of Newcastle immediately asked for the royal visit to be extended to include his city. By the time the visit was about to take place, a schedule of two full days of functions had been arranged and enormous preparations had been made in Newcastle, at the Docks and in the surrounding district. The details of this visit give a valid picture of the demands made upon Edward and how he responded to them.

On 19 August 1884 the royal party, consisting of the Prince, the Princess, his two sons and his suite, having travelled up by train from London the previous day, arrived at Newcastle's Central Railway Station, and were met by a large reception committee and a guard of honour of the First Northumberland Artillery Volunteers. A procession of forty carriages, escorted by mounted police and Northumberland Hussars formed up and proceeded on a long drive through the streets of Newcastle thronged with cheering crowds and decorated and illuminated as never before. The festive effect was stunning, as well it might have been, since between £2,000 and £3,000 had been raised, mainly by the merchants and tradespeople, to pay for these decorations. As the carriages passed St Nicholas's Cathedral 430 choristers positioned on the roof burst into the national anthem and the song which rivalled it in popularity: 'God Bless the Prince of Wales'. At one o'clock the procession finally reached the Banqueting Hall at Jesmond Dene where the first function, the opening of the Armstrong Public Park, took place. Addresses by the Recorder and the Prince, speech by the Mayor, opening ceremony by the Prince, planting of a tree by the Princess, presentation of illuminated Addresses, golden key and silver spade to the royal couple, all followed. The carriage procession formed up again and drove off, on a different route, through more cheering onlookers and festooned streets, to St George's Hall. Here luncheon was served to some 800 guests while a band played. In his toast to the Mayor and Corporation the Prince – who as usual spoke without notes – gracefully managed to include references to Newcastle's 'kind, cordial and northern welcome', to compare its friendliness with the brightness of the sun (the weather that day was lovely), to dwell briefly on the merits of the public works he had come to inaugurate and to congratulate the Mayor and Corporation on their admirable arrangements for his reception. This was joyfully received, all the guests rising and cheering and all the ladies waving their handkerchiefs. At four o'clock the party re-entered their carriages and moved off to the Natural History Museum which the Prince was to open. Here they were met by another guard of honour and a military band, and escorted round the Museum galleries where Edward performed the opening ceremony. Off went the party again to the final function, the opening of the Reference Department of the City's Public Library by the Prince. Another drive through crowds of spectators to the railway station and the ceremonies were concluded for the day.

On the next day the royal party were met at the station shortly before noon with a guard of honour and reception committee, the carriage procession formed up, drove through the streets of cheering spectators and down to the Fish Market. There they were welcomed by another guard of honour and a band, and the Chairman of the Tyne Commissioners who presented an Address to which the visitor replied. The royal party then embarked on a steamer which, followed by a long procession of ships carrying officials and guests, set off down the river, the sides of which were lined with cheering people and decorated boats. At half-past two, as Edward's steamer slowly entered the New Dock, cutting a ribbon stretched across the entrance, the Prince declared it open. To the roars of the huge crowd, the thunder of an artillery salute and the strains of 'God Bless the Prince of Wales', the royal party disembarked and walked to the pavilion where luncheon was laid for about 1,000 guests. The after-lunch speeches included one by Edward – again delivered impromptu – in which he contrived to thank and congratulate all concerned, to introduce interesting facts about the River Tyne and its shipping, to compare the sand-dredging necessary to deepen the river to that done in the Suez Canal (this brought enormous cheering), to observe that London still had nothing like the Tyne's Swing Bridge which he had seen that morning although the capital was hoping to copy it soon on the Thames (more cheers), to mention how much he had enjoyed the agreeable cruise and to express his pride in having his name associated with the New Dock. With cheering and fluttering of ladies' handkerchiefs the royal party embarked again on their steamer and sailed to Tynemouth where the Prince received and replied to Loyal Addresses from that community and four neighbouring towns and witnessed a display of rocket drill by the Tynemouth Volunteer Life Brigade. That evening he rounded off two busy days by inviting local dignitaries to dinner.

This detailed account of a two-day visit crammed with events gives some idea of Edward's stamina and expertise. He had driven for hours in an open carriage, smiling and lifting his hat continuously and at the same time noting things to which he referred in his speeches, inspected several guards of honour, shaken hundreds of hands, chatted pleasantly to local officials, delivered at least two impromptu speeches (and the Prince, who had a deep powerful voice, had taught himself the actor's art of 'throwing it' so as to be heard in every corner of a hall), and throughout it all had remained urbane and charming. His gratified hosts, who had already gleefully remarked, at the opening of the dock, upon the publicity value of his visit – 'It is known today all over England and over the world that the Prince has inaugurated this great work of improvement on the River Tyne' – were also left with the impression that he had been interested in everything and that he had enjoyed it all. At a Council meeting after the excitement was over, the Mayor of Newcastle was highly commended for having realised, as his Councillors put it, that the opening of a public park, a museum and a library department were objects that were likely to interest the Prince and Princess of Wales. These public duties, of which the Newcastle visit is an interesting sample, were performed all over the country. By the time of his accession, Edward was not only the first monarch to have been seen by a large proportion of his subjects, but he had firmly established the monarchy in this new role of public appearances.

The areas to benefit from these 'princely duties' were numerous. The Prince was interested in transport; he laid the foundation stone for London's Tower Bridge in 1886 and opened it eight years later. When the first 'Tube', the City and South London electric railway, was built to run from King William Street in the City to the south London suburb of Stockwell, it was Edward who performed the opening ceremony in 1890. He even favoured the idea of a Channel Tunnel to link England and France and went to Dover to inspect the preliminary workings in 1881. (Later he reluctantly agreed that this should be dropped in the interests of the country's defence.) He was interested in hotels and the prestige and trade they generated. Having sampled the luxurious

Edward opening London's 'Tube', the City and South London Railway, at Stockwell Station, 4 November 1890.
(London Transport Museum)

comfort of America's huge hotels on his New World tour in 1860, he associated himself, three years later, with London's first 'grand hotel', the Langham in Portland Place, by performing the opening ceremony.

Social service claimed Edward's attention when he was asked in 1884 by Gladstone, then Prime Minister, to serve as a member on the Royal Commission on Housing of the Working Classes. When a formal motion for the enrolment of this Commission was brought before the House of Lords on 2 March the Prince delivered a substantial speech, describing the improvements which he, as a landlord, had made to his labourers' cottages at Sandringham, and speaking with horror of the awful housing conditions he had seen in London during an incognito investigation. His interest in improved artisans' dwellings soon became widely known – it was alluded to approvingly by his hosts during his visit to Newcastle. It was on this Commission that Edward, when he proposed a lady, the social reformer Miss Octavia Hill, as a fellow member, showed himself to be more liberal and far-seeing than his horrified government colleagues. The Prince was far from being a feminist supporter and had scant sympathy later for the Suffragettes, but he did believe that women should participate, on a level with men, in social service. His female nominee was rejected, however, and appeared only as a witness. (Not until 1905, when Edward had become King, did he have the satisfaction of seeing Miss Hill appointed as one of the first women to serve as a full member of a Royal Commission.)

Museums were another area promoted by the Prince. He opened the Bethnal Green Museum in 1872, and in 1881 was invited to become a Trustee of the British Museum, where he fought hard for Sunday opening to enable working-men and their families to visit such establishments. In 1886 the House of Lords adopted this resolution, but it took the House of Commons another ten years to support his socially aware views and sanction this measure for the British Museum and other national institutions. In 1909, as King, he opened the Victoria and Albert Museum, whose foundation stone had been laid in 1899. This had been part of his father's grand design, formed after the 1851 Exhibition, to apply the profits from that successful enterprise to promote science, art and technology. Large tracts of land were purchased at Kensington, the district selected for this 'cultural estate'. After many vicissitudes the Government took over the building of the museums on the site, while the Royal Commission originally set up to be the administrator continued independently with its educational schemes.

Since his father's death the Prince had taken an active interest in the ambitious project; in 1870 he became president of the new Commission and in 1883 he appointed his erstwhile tutor and lifelong friend Professor Lyon Playfair, who had collaborated with Albert in 1851, to be its Honorary Secretary. Part of the Commission's brief had been the staging of Exhibitions. These manifestations of 'science and art', which to the public combined the pleasure of a good day's outing with the satisfying feeling of having participated in an educational experience, had become immensely popular. As a child Edward had been taken several times to his father's Great Exhibition, and as he grew up he was to visit many more and take a hand in their organisation. One such was the Colonies and India Exhibition (amusingly nicknamed 'The Colinderies' by the public), staged in London in 1886. For the impressive opening ceremony in May, Tennyson wrote an ode, set to music by Arthur Sullivan at the request of the Prince. The sentiments expressed in the verses exactly mirrored popular feeling at the time:

Britain's myriad voices call,
Sons, be welded each and all,
Into one imperial whole,
One with Britain, heart and soul!
One life, óne flag, one fleet, one Throne!
Britons, hold your own!

– a mix of pride, patriotism and the desire to be both the strongest and the most successful trading nation.

India in particular had come to hold a special place in the national consciousness and some of the credit for this was due to the Prince's successful 'Indian Tour' in 1875–6. This project, which developed into one of the Prince's most impressive public appearances, did not get off to a very good start. Victoria was unenthusiastic, the Government uncertain. One stumbling-block was the relative prestige of the Viceroy of India, Lord Northbrook, the Queen's representative, and that of the heir to the throne. Who would take precedence when they appeared together? Victoria favoured the Viceroy; Lord Salisbury, India Office Secretary, came down on the Prince's side. After a sharp tussle, a compromise was reached: Edward would hold levees, and the huge Durbar planned under his presidency (normally the prerogative of the Viceroy) would be re-named a special Chapter of the Star of India. This obstacle overcome, a new one surfaced. Who was going to pay for what would obviously be an expensive trip, including, as a very necessary item, the presents which the Prince would have to offer to the Indian Maharajahs? Rumours were already reaching Britain of the fabulous preparations and gifts being got ready for the Prince in India (these were to surpass expectations). Prime Minister Disraeli eventually got funds voted through the House of Commons – £52,000 to the Admiralty to transport the Prince, £30,000 for the Viceroy to provide suitable entertainment, £60,000 for Edward's expenses and to pay for the much-discussed presents (public opinion, which had been deploring the cost of the trip, now felt that the amount was 'shabby' and that the Prince would not be able to make a good show with his presents). Over the remaining area of dispute, that of who was to be taken in his suite, the Queen fought a spirited rear-guard action. But, with Disraeli's intervention, the matter was settled amicably and the party, led by Sir Bartle Frere of the India Office, finally included three of Edward's personal friends as well as the necessary equerries and aides-de-camp, chaplain and doctor, the reporter from *The Times* W H Russell, the artist Sydney Prior Hall, and Clarence Bartlett, assistant-superintendent of London's Zoological Gardens as taxidermist on the tour. Victoria contented herself with impressing upon her thirty-three-year-old son the necessity for being careful with his diet (his three chefs travelled with the party) and going to bed every night at ten o'clock.

The party set off overland to Brindisi on Monday 11 October 1875. The previous day the Prince's friend Arthur Stanley had emphasised in his sermon in Westminster Abbey the interest aroused by the first journey to India ever undertaken by an heir to the throne. Lying at Brindisi were HMS *Serapis*, a white-painted, specially converted troopship, two frigates and the Royal Yacht *Osborne*. The flotilla set off, and after brief stops at Athens (where Edward spent a day with his brother-in-law the King of Greece), Cairo and Aden, reached Bombay on 8 November. As the *Serapis* steamed slowly into the harbour between two lines of British battleships, guns fired, bands played and the Prince stood on the bridge acknowledging the salutes. At the dock he was met by the Town Council reception committee and some seventy Indian chiefs and princes with their entourages. Huge crowds cheered his procession to Government House.

The Prince's visit to India, 1875–6. Edward receiving a garland at a fete for schoolchildren in Bombay, November 1875.
(The *Illustrated London News* Picture Library)

Edward's entry into Baroda with the Maharanee, November 1875.
(The *Illustrated London News* Picture Library)

The Prince was immediately plunged into a whirl of public appearances which lasted for seventeen weeks. Despite his mother's fears he was in splendid health, unaffected by the alterations in climate and full of energy. His thirty-fourth birthday was celebrated in festive style in Bombay, decorated and illuminated for the occasion. Cheerful, friendly and patriotic banners, some of them inscribed 'How is your Royal Mother?' and 'Tell Mama we're happy', greeted him as he drove through the town. Encouraged and gratified by this enthusiastic reception, Sir Bartle Frere and his other advisers arranged a weekend trip to nearby Baroda, a state in which the effects of the recent deposing of a corrupt ruler and his replacement by a new ruler or Gaekwar in the person of the twelve-year-old foster-son of the Maharanee, a previous Gaekwar's widow, were still being felt. It was hoped that the Prince's visit would calm the situation, and so it proved. Edward entered Baroda at the head of a huge procession, riding in a golden howdah on a gorgeously caparisoned and painted elephant with the Maharanee, a cultured lady who had abandoned the custom of wearing the veil. He was greeted by the eager little ruler laden with jewels, and treated to an entertainment which included some exciting hunting and shooting and staged 'wild beast fights'. (Edward wrote home to his small son George about these fights of elephants, rhinoceros and buffaloes against each other, assuring him that none got hurt, except for one poor buffalo who had his horn broken.)

Everyone, his advisers and Indians alike, was delighted with the Prince and the way he handled the situation. Sir Bartle, who had an extensive knowledge of India, was particularly struck by the way the royal visitor employed the same affable and charming manner to all classes of Indians, from the little Gaekwar and the Maharanee to the old native regimental officers presented to him. Edward, in fact, though fascinated by the new surroundings in which he

Edward in Calcutta, during December 1875–January 1876. Edward and an audience of British officials and Indian princes and officials being entertained by Indian music and dancing at a garden party.
(The *Illustrated London News* Picture Library)

found himself, had been keeping his eyes open and had already reported to his mother on the 'rude and rough' manner of some British officials towards the Indian chiefs, strongly criticising this behaviour and adding: 'Natives of all classes in this country will, I am sure, be more attached to us if they are treated with kindness and with firmness at the same time, but not with brutality or contempt.' A few days later he was writing: 'Because a man has a black face and a different religion from our own, there is no reason why he should be treated as a brute.' These liberal observations were received sympathetically by the Prime Minister, by Lord Salisbury and by the Queen herself, who in this respect held views similar to those of her son, and in time were acted upon.

The Prince, meanwhile, was indefatigably continuing with his public appearances. On 1 December the party arrived in Ceylon; the round of official functions was enlivened by a big elephant shoot from a camp set up outside Colombo. In the midst of a sudden charge by the animals, Edward 'bagged' one elephant and severely wounded two others, as he telegraphed triumphantly to his anxious mother. Crossing to the mainland to view the temples and palaces of the Madura region, the party went on to another huge welcome in Madras and six days crammed with functions, including a big review of troops. The Prince was also treated to an unusual entertainment, 'the illumination of the surf'. As the visitors watched from the pier around which the surf was crashing, from far out at sea great balls of fire came suddenly flashing and burning through the rollers; instantly masses of little boats launched themselves from the shore, riding the blazing surf, turning and dashing back to the pier, an awesome and exciting spectacle which lasted well into the night. The journey to Calcutta was made by sea. To thunderous gun-salutes from all the ships and land forts, the Prince, in full-dress Field Marshal's uniform ablaze with orders, landed on Christmas Eve to find all the gorgeously bedecked rulers of northern India waiting to greet him and present gifts. A week full of brilliant functions followed – levees, visits and receptions. On New Year's Day 12,000 spectators gathered to watch the specially-arranged Chapter of the Star of India over which the Prince presided in a ceremony full of pageantry, rounded off by polo matches, fireworks and a banquet.

On 4 January Edward set off on a long tour through northern India, a tour which became a triumphal progress. A continuous stream of reports was being sent home to the Queen, the Prime Minister and the India Office as all the officials in the touring party as well as those in India rushed to put pen to paper, and the consensus was an enthusiastic acclaim of the Prince's success. Lord Napier, in charge of a huge military camp assembled at Delhi, where the royal visitor had reviewed some 18,000 Indian troops and then watched them engage in a well-staged sham battle, told the Queen: 'His Royal Highness's manner and bearing have realised their [the Indians'] idea of a Prince.' Sir Henry Dale, Agent for the vast area of central India through which the Prince had passed, reported: 'The effect of the Prince on the Chiefs is miraculous . . . he listens to tales of service with an air of interest and wins his way.' And Sir Bartle Frere, summing up the tour for the Queen, told her that Edward, who had behaved perfectly throughout, had won the affection of India's people by making them feel that he stood in just the same relationship to them as to the British. These feelings were reinforced at Delhi when the title of 'The Prince of Wales' Own' was conferred on four Indian regiments and the Prince had the happy notion of inviting two rissaldars (Indian cavalry officers) to join his suite for the remainder of the tour (at their own request they accompanied him home and stayed in London for a few months' holiday).

Indian animals brought home by Edward on the *Serapis*. (Left) Sailors on deck watching a young tiger being exercised. (Right) A midshipman giving the Himalayan black bear a bath, watched by the tail-less dogs.
(The *Illustrated London News* Picture Library)

As the visitor progressed across northern India the rulers vied with each other to offer him opportunities for big-game hunting. This resulted in some exciting days, as the Prince wrote to his little sons from Nepal: 'I have had great tiger shooting. The day before yesterday I killed six and some were very savage. Two were man-eaters. Today I killed a tigress and she had a little cub with her.' He told his boys that he hoped to bring some cubs home with him, and so he did, not only tiger cubs but a whole menagerie of live, and dead, animals. When the *Serapis*, resplendent with fresh white paint and re-gilding, finally steamed out of Bombay harbour on 13 March 1876 on her homeward journey, not only did her holds contain a veritable treasury of priceless gifts from the Indian Princes, but her decks were crowded with, among other specimens, four elephants (two of them only 6 feet high), seven leopards, a swift little cheetah, five tigers (including one cub no bigger than a cat), a grey Arab horse, a Himalayan bear, tail-less dogs and three ostriches, giving her the appearance of a Noah's Ark. And below decks Mr Bartlett, the Prince's taxidermist, was busy stuffing his hunting trophies.

Edward finally reached home on 11 May. The triumphant conclusion of his tour was slightly marred for the Prince by the fact that he had been sent no official notification but had been left to find out from the newspapers that the title of Empress of India had been conferred upon his mother. Since the timing of this government decision was due in part to his success in India, and since as heir to the throne the Imperial title would ultimately descend upon himself, he felt this undeserved snub keenly. But the public, who had been following all his Indian adventures in the illustrated papers, gave him an enthusiastic welcome. Landing at Portsmouth and taken by special train to London, he drove to Marlborough House through cheering crowds and within an hour of getting there was off with the Princess to the opera where he received a standing ovation and a rendering of 'God Bless the Prince of Wales' from the stage before the performance began, and ovations again between the acts.

Edward's attendance at the opera on that particular evening was in the nature of a public appearance, it being deemed his duty to show himself after such a long absence. But opera was also one of his passions – indeed a 'princely pleasure' – and the opera performed that night, Verdi's *Un Ballo in Maschera*, one of his favourites. His first visit was at the age of nine, on 8 April 1851, when he was taken to Covent Garden for Auber's *Massaniello*, and during his stay in Rome in 1859 he was allowed to attend the opera on several occasions, going twice to Bellini's *Norma*. The last opera he attended, a few days before he died, was Wagner's *Siegfried* at Covent Garden.

Victoria and Albert, themselves very musical, had encouraged their son's interest in opera, an interest which soon extended to music in general. The Prince believed that the cultivation and appreciation of music not only gave pleasure but that common enjoyment by all classes could help to overcome mutual jealousies and misunderstandings. In 1875 he helped to found a training school of music offering fifty free scholarships. The following year he worked energetically to get the school expanded into a Royal College of Music; by 1883 he had succeeded and opened this institution, in South Kensington near the Albert Hall, with the stirring words: 'Class can no longer stand apart from class . . . I claim for music that it produces that union of feeling which I much desire to promote.' As the Royal College of Music grew in importance Edward laid the foundation stone for an extension in 1890 and performed its opening ceremony in 1894. But he did not enjoy music only in the capital; he regularly attended provincial festivals. From Sandringham he often went to

the Norwich Music Festival; there in 1884 he heard Gounod's *Redemption*, declaring that it was 'admirably given and the music was exceptionally fine'. And he was associated with the Leeds Festival of which Arthur Sullivan had been appointed Artistic Director and Conductor in 1880.

The Prince had met Sullivan in 1863 when the promising young composer had contributed his *Princess of Wales's March* to his wedding festivities. The two became friends and Sullivan became a member of Edward's set. It may have been through the agency of the Prince that Sullivan received his knighthood: at the composer's birthday party in May 1883 Edward playfully told his host that 'something significant' was in store for him; nine days later he was knighted at Windsor by the Queen. Sullivan is perhaps best known today for his collaboration with the librettist W S Gilbert in their sparkling 'Savoy Operas' whose catchy tunes provided the repertoire for many a brass and military band and which were all the rage from about 1881 on. (Their popularity had not waned when the Prince became King. In 1907 *The Mikado* was playing when the imminent state visit of a Japanese prince caused the Lord Chamberlain's Office to have it taken off, thus provoking an outcry. Gilbert, furious at the loss of his royalties, at first believed that this order had come from the King himself, but on being assured that it had come from the Japanese visitor, he commented that Edward's well-known sense of humour should have made the public realise that he could not be responsible. Immediately the visitor left, *The Mikado* was on again.) But Sullivan was also a serious musician and undertook many royal commissions, including anthems for funerals at the Royal Mausoleum at Frogmore and, to celebrate Victoria's Diamond Jubilee in 1897, a patriotic composition, *Victoria and Merrie England*, first performed at the Alhambra Theatre in May of that year, accompanied by eight tableaux vivants on the stage.

This form of entertainment, a favourite of the Queen's, had been part of the Prince's childhood and from it may have partly stemmed his great love of the theatre. The tableau vivant consisted of 'making a picture' with human actors, actors who neither moved nor spoke but were 'frozen' into immobility. The effect aimed at was for the tableau to 'tell a story', in the manner of the popular painted pictures of the period and their imitators just coming into fashion, the 'story-photographs'. One of Sullivan's tableaux at the Alhambra was 'The coronation of Queen Victoria' which obviously required an elaborate set and costumes. But this was customary, even for tableaux vivants performed at home before an audience consisting only of friends and relations. That this form of 'home-made' entertainment was thought impressive enough even for royal visitors was evidently the opinion of the Earl and Countess of Fife when they welcomed the newly married Edward and Alexandra to Mar Lodge in 1863. The tableaux put on for that occasion, repeatedly and warmly applauded by the royal couple and subsequently preserved and 'documented' through the medium of photography, included a mix of historical, moral, symbolic and romantic subjects: 'Mary Queen of Scots and her secretary Rizzio', 'Charlotte Corday (Marat's assassin) before her execution', 'Faith, Hope and Charity' and 'The Soldier's Return'. The confused linkage between painted pictures and tableaux vivants was much in evidence at a charity show of tableaux organised by Lady Freke at her house in South Kensington. The idea was that each tableau would be 'directed' by a leading painter and would depict one of his best-known masterpieces. The artist Millais selected his picture *Effie Deane* (a character in Sir Walter Scott's novel *The Heart of Midlothian*) and chose to represent the heroine the beautiful Lillie Langtry. Mrs Langtry was posed by Millais, as in his picture, leaning over a stile, taking leave of her seducer and holding in her hand the symbol of her maidenhood – the snood traditionally worn by young girls – which she no longer had the right to wear; the pathetic tableau was much appreciated by the audience.

All this activity demonstrates the eternal desire of many adults to indulge in 'dressing-up', and nowhere was this more in evidence than in the fancy-dress balls which became a veritable 'princely pleasure'. In 1871 the Prince and Princess attended the Waverley Ball, held to commemorate the centenary of Sir Walter Scott, at which all the guests had to dress as characters from his ever-popular 'Waverley novels'. Alexandra chose to go as 'Mary Queen of Scots', but rather as the beautiful and desirable woman depicted by Scott in *The Abbot* than as the tragic martyr of history. Her dress, therefore, was not the sombre black robe usually associated with the Scottish Queen, but a glowing confection of claret-red velvet. She was escorted by Edward dressed, as the gallant character of 'Lord of the Isles' from Scott's long poem of that name, in kilt, breast-plate, mailed gloves and feathered bonnet, hung about with two pistols, broadsword and hunting horn and with a dirk stuck into the top of his knee-sock. (Lord of the Isles was one of the Prince's own inherited Scottish titles.)

The success of the Waverley Ball and the fun of dressing-up must have appealed to the royal couple since three years later, in July 1874, they gave a fancy-dress ball of their own at Marlborough House. This brilliant event was meticulously planned by Edward who asked his artist friend Frederic Leighton to supervise the decorations. The result astounded the 1,400 guests who danced until dawn. Supper was taken in two huge scarlet marquees, one hung with tapestries and furnished with suits of armour, the other displaying magnificent Indian carpets. The dresses were as sumptuous as the setting. The

H.R.H. The Prince of Wales
AS LORD OF THE ISLES.
PHOTOGRAPHED BY ROYAL COMMAND & PUBLISHED BY SPECIAL PERMISSION

Alexandra dressed as Mary Queen of Scots
for the Waverley Ball in 1871.
(Scottish National Portrait Gallery,
Edinburgh; photographer unknown)

Edward dressed as Lord of the Isles for the
Waverley Ball in 1871.
(National Portrait Gallery, London;
photograph by A J Melhuish)

Prince was in a Van Dyck costume of maroon satin embroidered in gold; his cloak was clasped on the shoulder with a huge diamond star. Men and ladies alike were smothered in jewels. Alexandra, who may have had her Waverley dress re-modelled into what was called the sixteenth-century Venetian style, covered the bodice with strings of pearls and had sparkling gems sewn all down the front panel. Ideas for costumes were culled from many sources, historical characters, painted pictures, fairy-tales and novels among others. The costumes at the Devonshire House Ball in 1897, organised to celebrate Victoria's Diamond Jubilee, were similarly inspired. This ball, at which Edward and Alexandra were the principal guests, may well have been the most elaborate of the age. It almost took on the nature of a pageant with guests planning and practising their processions and dances for weeks beforehand and famous couturiers being called upon to design and make the superb costumes. Alexandra went as Marguerite de Valois, first wife of the French King Henry IV, in a sumptuous gown with a huge stiffened ruff-collar, embellished with her customary choker necklace and stomacher and endless cascades, swags and *sautoirs* of pearls. With an unerring sense of theatre the Prince, as the Grand Prior of the Order of St John of Jerusalem, attired himself almost entirely in black – velvet doublet and hose, cloak of cut velvet, long leather boots and high feathered hat – a focal point in the crowded ballroom and a stately foil to the multi-coloured throng.

The theatre proper was one of Edward's greatest 'princely pleasures'. His parents, educatively enlightened in this respect, had encouraged him, and all their children, to 'dress up', perform tableaux vivants and act little plays in the schoolroom. Recitations in French and German, as well as English, were

Edward dressed as the Grand Prior of the Order of St John of Jerusalem for the Devonshire House Ball in 1897.
(National Portrait Gallery, London; photograph by Lafayette)

encouraged; as a small boy he recited pieces from Racine and Schiller and acted and recited the part of Winter – wearing a huge white beard and a cloak covered in 'icicles' – in a dramatisation of Thomson's poem 'The Seasons'. And from the age of seven he was able to watch successive troupes of 'real actors' performing at Court on his mother's invitation; his twelfth birthday was celebrated with a special performance of Shakespeare's *Henry V* at Windsor. Visits to the theatre remained one of Edward's pleasures throughout his life, wherever he found himself (in Calcutta he and the Viceroy found time to see a performance of a popular farce played by a London company on tour in India). He often arranged private performances at Sandringham for his guests. When Victoria visited him there in April 1889 he invited the distinguished actor-manager, Henry Irving, doyen of the profession, to perform for her the melodrama *The Bells*, as well as the trial scene from *The Merchant of Venice* with the leading actress, Ellen Terry. The Prince's interest in the stage was both professional – as Sir Lionel Cust noted, he carefully observed, and assimilated, acting techniques – and personal. He made friends of many outstanding members of the theatrical profession, meeting them in the Garrick Club and raising their social standing by admitting them to Society. It was possibly through his agency that the theatre was officially honoured in 1895 with the bestowing of a knighthood on Henry Irving.

When in 1881 Mrs Langtry was in social and financial difficulties and, perhaps encouraged by her success in the tableaux, sought a way out of her embarrassments in an acting career, the Prince called upon his theatre friends to help her. Their response was generous. Mrs Langtry was launched in a charity performance of *She Stoops to Conquer* which, Edward informed his son George, was a great success, and was then taken on by the actor and actress/managers team of Mr and Mrs Squire Bancroft who controlled two London theatres. They gave her the leading role in *Ours*, a play about the Crimean War; Edward went to see it three times with parties of friends and got her career off to a triumphant start. As a gesture of thanks to his theatre friends the Prince arranged a big, much publicised and acclaimed dinner party at Marlborough House on 19 February 1882. The guest list was an interesting mix of members of the theatrical profession, including Irving and Bancroft, and writers, including George Augustus Sala, novelist and journalist who had reported the 1870 Franco-Prussian War for the *Daily Telegraph*, and George Grossmith, co-author of *Diary of a Nobody* whose talents as an actor were displayed in many of Gilbert and Sullivan's Savoy Operas, together with members of 'Edwardian Society'. Mrs Langtry's subsequent acting career, which included a tour of the United States in 1882–3, brought this courageous beauty success, happiness and wealth, so much so that in a few years' time she was able to indulge in a hobby which she shared with the Prince, by becoming a race-horse owner.

Horses had always been one of Edward's pleasures. He learned to ride at the age of five and continued for most of his life, hunted at fifteen and again as an undergraduate, and in America, after watching with interest a sport new to him, bought himself a trotting-horse. After his marriage he kept a large stable at Sandringham, generously providing mounts for his guests. He loved to go

Edward VII riding his horse Iron Duke in November 1906.
(National Portrait Gallery, London; photograph by J Russell and Sons)

round the stables on a Sunday afternoon, chatting to his head groom, inspecting his horses, indulging them with carrots and sugar-lumps. He became interested in racing when he was elected a member of the Jockey Club in 1864 and began to attend the big race meetings. But it was not until after his return from India that he became an owner and entered the first horse to carry the royal colours of purple, gold braid, scarlet sleeves and black velvet cap with gold fringe at Newmarket in July 1877. He appointed Lord Marcus Beresford (younger brother of Lord Charles) as his racing manager and extended his stable to include entrants for flat racing as well as steeplechasing. Lord Marcus established a stud at Sandringham with a mare named Perdita II. Her offspring were to give the Prince notable racing triumphs. In 1896 one of them, Persimmon, won both the Derby and the St Leger, and in 1900 Persimmon's brother, Diamond Jubilee, won the amazing total of all five classic races (the Two Thousand Guineas, the Newmarket Stakes, the Eclipse Stakes, the Derby and the St Leger). Edward's racing career was followed closely by the public and his successes applauded. Many of his subjects were excited by what he called 'the glorious uncertainty of the turf'. They liked a day at the races, they liked to 'have a flutter' – and they liked a Prince who felt the same way.

During the forty years spent 'in waiting' for the throne Edward's 'princely duties' produced an unforeseen result; they made him into a figure with whom a vast number of his future subjects became familiar, a phenomenon which had never occurred before. Through the increasing spread of the photograph, his image was already well known; his indefatigable round of appearances allowed multitudes to see him 'in the flesh'. Even his 'princely pleasures' contributed to this result, since many of them, for example theatre-going and racing, were conducted in public. Once the republican agitation had somewhat abated, the monarchy began to take on a new look in the person of the Prince of Wales. He came to personify a dual aspect – the dignified future King, and the human being on a par with the public, with the same zest for life, the same enjoyments, and the same weaknesses and faults. Edward's way of life corresponded in reality to that of only a small section of society and did not mirror the conditions of a large part of the population who were struggling with uncongenial and ill-paid jobs, inadequate housing, poor health and an uncertain future. But, in a limited way and as far as he was allowed, the Prince, tirelessly going round the country and getting an overview denied to many politicians, promoted trade and industry, encouraged educational opportunities through the media of exhibitions, museums and art galleries, supported projects in hospitals and nursing, spoke out strongly against racialism and tried to weaken the rigid class structure through the introduction of common interests such as music.

As the century wore on and Edward's accession to the throne became imminent, the public began to ask themselves what would happen when the familiar figure of their Prince became that of the monarch. Would he change? Would he shut himself up in Windsor and live as remote from the people as his mother had done? And added to these questions was another. Would it mean the end of his trips to the Continent, and especially to his beloved France?

7

A LIFELONG LOVE AFFAIR WITH FRANCE

*E*DWARD'S love affair with France began in his childhood and lasted all his life. When he grew up hardly a year passed without a visit – a few days in Paris, a stay on the Riviera. France's fears that the Prince she had known and entertained for forty years would desert her when he became King proved to be unfounded. His affection never faltered, and after a period of political estrangement occasioned by the Boer War, Edward triumphantly brought Britain and France together in the *Entente Cordiale*. France was the last country he visited, saying goodbye sadly as he left a mere ten days before his death: 'I shall be sorry to leave Biarritz . . . perhaps for good.'

It was in August 1855 that the thirteen-year-old Edward first saw the country, and its capital, which were to hold a lasting fascination for him. He accompanied his parents on a visit to Louis-Napoleon, then Emperor of the French as Napoleon III. This nephew of Napoleon Bonaparte had had a turbulent career. Attempting to revive the Bonapartist legend, he had twice tried to overthrow the reigning King Louis-Philippe, scion of the Orleanist branch of the former French royal family. When the latter fell in the revolution of 1848, Louis-Napoleon was voted into power as President. A further *coup d'état* and two more plebiscites made him Emperor of the French in 1852. At first regarded with suspicion by Britain, by 1855 he was accepted, and Victoria's visit was made to cement the new Anglo-French understanding. The young Prince's first view of Paris, therefore, was of a city in festive mood, gay with decorations and ready to make much of its royal visitors. The Parisians were especially intrigued by the boy Prince, in full Highland dress, escorting his mother on sightseeing outings. They went together to the Hôtel des Invalides to pay homage at the tomb of Napoleon (whose remains had been brought back from St Helena in 1840). This visit took place at night; tall old men, former Guards in Napoleon's army, held up torches to light the crypt and a thunderstorm crashed and pealed overhead as the Prince knelt beside the huge red granite tomb of his great-grandfather's bitter enemy with its simple inscription: 'Let my ashes lie beside the Seine among the French people I have loved so well.' It was an impressive and dramatic scene which brought tears to the eyes of the French generals in the party. One brilliant reception followed another: the Imperial hunt in the forest of St Germain, a large ball at Versailles where a firework display included a set-piece of Windsor Castle and where Edward's graceful dancing was admired by the observant French. The dazzling effect of this visit on the impressionable young boy was never effaced; a lasting relationship had been forged, and although shaken from time to time by political upheavals, only death broke the link.

The Prince's extensive travels as a young man left him little time to indulge his preference for France; but on the way home from his Middle-East tour in 1862 he managed to stop over in Paris, visit the Emperor and his Empress Eugenie at Fontainebleau and, having discovered the delights of Parisian shops, buy some 'pretty things' for Alexandra, his fiancée-to-be. In the years after his marriage it gradually became Edward's custom to visit France in early spring, travelling down to the Riviera and spending a few days in Paris on the way there and back. These were the years of the Second Empire and its glittering Court, when Paris was the acknowledged centre of elegance and

A fashion design by Charles Frederic Worth, who became one of the most influential dress designers in Paris.
(Bibliothèque des Arts Décoratifs, Paris; photograph by Lauros-Giraudon)

Hortense Schneider, French singer and actress who appeared in many of Jacques Offenbach's operettas, shown here in the leading role of his *La Grande Duchesse de Gerolstein.*

fashion. Edward and Alexandra sampled the wares of the French couturiers in May 1869 as they passed through Paris on their way home from a winter cruise taken to restore Alexandra's health after the birth of her fourth child. Between the excitements of a military review and a ball given for the Princess by the Emperor, the young couple found time to choose two dresses. On their arrival in Paris the Prince had received a scolding letter about expenses from Victoria, who added: 'I hope dear Alix [Alexandra's nickname] will not spend much on dress in Paris'. To this 'jobation' he replied coolly: 'You need not be afraid, dear Mama, that Alix will commit any extravagances with regard to dress, etc. I have given her two simple ones, as they make them here better than in London; but if there is anything I dislike, it is extravagant or outré dresses' (although he somewhat spoiled his dignified reproach by adding, 'at any rate, in my wife'). Edward did not mention from which couturier he had made his purchases. It may have been from the Englishman, Charles Frederic Worth, who came from the small village of Bourne in Lincolnshire to establish himself as one of the leading Parisian dressmakers. Worth was patronised by the Empress Eugenie and other royal ladies; in 1875 he invented for Alexandra the 'Princess line' – a smooth, close-fitting style which set off her slim figure to perfection.

On this particular visit Alexandra was with Edward, but usually he travelled to France alone, taking with him only a small entourage. His days in Paris were crowded and pleasurable. He put up in hotels, often the Hôtel Bristol in the Place Vendôme, always occupying the same suite. On arrival he consulted the theatre guides and made a selection. At the theatres he always had two boxes on the ground floor thrown into one and furnished with a comfortable chair. Pre-1870 Parisian theatre was dominated by the operettas of Jacques Offenbach. This German-born composer had left Paris during the 1848 revolution, but returned in the wake of Louis-Napoleon, soon to become Emperor. His gay, light-hearted and witty compositions came to stand as a symbol of the Second Empire, with its elegance and style, its reckless gaiety, its feverish pursuit of pleasure. Offenbach's leading ladies were acclaimed by all, including the Prince. One of his favourites was Hortense Schneider who, in the 1860s, played the lead in *La Grande Duchesse de Gerolstein*. Perhaps, when Bismarck saw this operetta, with its mocking look at militarism, he may have realised that France would fall an easy prey to a Prussian attack. In any event, so it proved: in 1870 Bismarck stamped out the Second Empire and its gaiety and sent the Imperial family into exile.

The Prince, bound to France by affection and to Germany by family ties, in his dismay at the crushing French defeat and the heavy casualty lists on both sides, offered to mediate. But in the event all he could do was to offer the exiled Empress Eugenie and her son a house near London (she refused this offer and settled near Chislehurst) and to pay her, and the Emperor when he was finally allowed to join his wife, friendly visits of sympathy. In February 1871 the British Government officially recognised the Third French Republic. Edward, however, found it hard to reconcile himself to French republican sentiments. In 1872, after his severe illness, when he visited France for the first time since the Franco-Prussian War, the Government requested that he pay a call on the President of the Republic, M. Thiers. He was very reluctant to do this, telling the Foreign Secretary that it went 'very much against the grain'. But he gave in gracefully and was received by the President with open arms. He resumed his visits to France, gradually extending his circle of acquaintances to include not only Imperialist and Orleanist adherents but also Republicans.

The opportunity to get on terms with the country's new rulers presented itself when France decided to stage a huge International Exhibition in Paris to open in spring 1878. The Prince was invited by the French Government to be President of the British section, and he agreed, knowing that his participation would be understood as an acceptance of the Republic as an expression of the French national will. He threw himself energetically into the work of assembling a worthwhile British contribution. He arranged for the election of his

Edward met Alexandre Gustave Eiffel (1832–1923), the French engineer, in 1889. The Prince was invited to contribute his expertise to the Paris International Exhibition in that year, but declined on the grounds that the Exhibition, planned to celebrate the centenary of the 1789 French Revolution, was overtly anti-monarchical. Nevertheless, he paid a private visit during which Eiffel personally conducted him over his engineering masterpiece, the much talked-about Eiffel Tower, then the highest building in the world and the centrepiece of the Exhibition. (National Portrait Gallery, London; photograph by Walery)

Sarah Bernhardt (right) with Mrs Lillie Langtry in America, where these two friends of Edward were enjoying successful theatrical tours. The ladies decided to be photographed together, but posing was difficult since Sarah was in a merry mood, making everyone laugh. The photographer caught the moment when the 'Jersey Lily' turned her head in surprise to look at the mischievous Sarah who had pinched her arm. (By courtesy of the Board of Trustees of the Victoria & Albert Museum; photograph by Sarony)

artist friend Frederic Leighton as President of the International Jury of Paintings; he persuaded owners of English School pictures to lend them; he sought the help and advice of his friend Professor Lyon Playfair and personally encouraged British manufacturers to send exhibits. He travelled back and forth to Paris and when the British pavilion was set up he supervised all the detailed arrangements. In March 1878 Edward wrote to his mother from the Hôtel Bristol: 'I find I shall have a great deal to do with the Exhibition.' Two days before the opening he invited all the members of the British Commission to a grand luncheon at the Café de la Paix. After the opening ceremony at the Trocadéro on 1 May, where he had been a prominent figure – laughingly responding to playful shouts of 'Vive la République!' from some French deputies – he wrote triumphantly to Victoria that his hard work had been 'amply rewarded by the greatest success of the British section, which is almost entirely complete, and no other country, not even France, can say the same. I think I have seen everything we have to show and talked with almost every exhibitor', adding an interesting comment on this manifestation of France's efforts to rekindle national enthusiasm and well-being: 'the Exhibition as a whole, that is as far as I can judge, is very fine and quite immense and endless what one has to see ... the money that has been spent is quite incredible and shows what a rich country this is'. And the Prince, as he had determined to do, saluted the Republic at a banquet given by the British exhibitors on 3 May at the Hôtel du Louvre. To the large assembly, which included many French notables, he spoke, in English and French and as usual without notes, on the mutual interests of Britain and France and the friendly participation engendered by the Exhibition. His speeches were greeted with great applause and widely reported in both countries. The success of the British pavilion was universally attributed to his energy and organising ability and the current popularity of Britain to his genial presence.

The Prince's chance to become acquainted with a leading French republican, Léon Gambetta, came at a dinner party at the Quai d'Orsay (the French

Foreign Office). Gambetta's daring exploit, at the height of Bismarck's siege of Paris in 1870, of escaping in a balloon to try to raise resistance to the Prussian armies, had made headlines. The unprepossessing manner and careless appearance of this colourful character had not previously impressed the Prince, but he did find conversation with him interesting and subsequently met the ardent republican several times. One of their good-humoured discussions over a convivial supper at the Café Anglais dealt with the relative role of aristocracy and nobility in their respective countries, Gambetta affirming that a republic could not have an aristocracy, that merit was its own reward and needed no title, the Prince expressing his preference for a nobility of men of talent rather than an aristocracy based entirely on hereditary rights. It was this staunch republican, whose premature death put an end to a promising friendship, who succinctly analysed his royal friend's feeling for his country when he said: 'The Prince loves France at once *gaiement et sérieusement*' (light-heartedly and yet deeply). Gambetta's further observation that the Prince's 'dream of the future is an *entente* with us' was not to become reality until Edward became King.

Throughout the intervening years the Prince was often to be seen strolling along the Paris boulevards, shopping, visiting artists' studios, going to the races at Longchamp, spending jolly evenings at the Jockey Club and even jollier ones in the Parisian music halls, popular centres of entertainment for all classes whose cabaret artistes have been immortalised in the paintings of Toulouse-Lautrec. A story that one of these ladies, nicknamed La Goulue, had cheekily called out as Edward entered with his party "Allo, Wales! Are you going to buy me a glass of champagne?' raised some eyebrows in London. But at the Moulin-Rouge itself, the Prince's deep amused laugh and his quick call for 'Champagne all round!' were well received by the crowded room. The Paris theatres were always on his programme. When he resumed his visits after the Franco-Prussian War the rising theatrical star was Sarah Bernhardt, 'the divine Sarah' as she came to be known from the emotional intensity of her acting and the effect she had upon her audience, including him. While she was in London in 1879, playing Racine's *Phèdre* at the Gaiety Theatre, a charity fete was organised in aid of the French Hospital. Madame Sarah took a stall, at which the Prince was an early, and constant customer; among the items he purchased was an oil painting of Sarah herself.

When he ascended the throne, and after the breach caused by the Boer War had been healed, Edward's visits to France and to the Paris theatres continued as before; in Parisian eyes only his title had changed, from 'Le Prince' to 'Le Roi'. This led to an amusing incident in 1909, which illustrates both his sense of humour and French appreciation of him as 'the most Parisian of royals'. Edward announced his intention of going to the Théâtre des Variétés to see a humorous satire, *Le Roi*, by Robert de Flers and Gaston de Caillavet. Authors and theatre management were aghast, since in their production a photograph of Edward himself was prominently displayed on the stage in somewhat compromising circumstances. One of the characters in the play, a famous actress, is asked by the French Government to entertain a 'Ruritanian' King as she had done during his visit seven years before; the 'Ruritanian' arrives and declares that his memory of their previous encounter has never faded; she replies coyly that he has never left her and points to a large photograph on her table, whereupon the 'Ruritanian' exclaims in dismay, 'But that is a photo of my uncle, the King of England!'. As Edward sat in his box at the theatre, the whole house waited in trepidation for this scene; but they need not have

The Hôtel du Palais at Biarritz, which
Edward visited regularly: (above) the
King's private drawing-room, (above left)
the great entrance hall, (left) the King's
bedroom.
(By kind permission of the Director-
General of the Hôtel du Palais, Biarritz)

feared – he was neither affronted nor embarrassed but laughed uproariously to
the immense delight of the audience. The King's last visit to a Paris theatre
was on 7 March 1910 to see Edmond Rostand's *Chantecler*. Sadly it was not
enjoyable; he wrote to his son George; 'I was dreadfully disappointed with
Chantecler. I never saw anything so stupid and childish and more like a
pantomime' – the actors, representing birds, were dressed in feathered
costumes.

Paris was the hub of Edward's visits, but it was also the starting-point for
his trips to the South. In the early years his preference was for Nice and
Cannes. His visits were usually in spring and he sometimes participated in the
Carnival festivities which marked the beginning of Lent. He was often asked
to perform civic ceremonies; in 1898 he laid the foundation stone of a new jetty
at Cannes, using the occasion to call for better understanding between France
and Britain. When he became King he abandoned the Riviera, choosing
instead the resort of Biarritz on the south-west coast. He put up at the Hôtel du
Palais, the sumptuous building which had once been the seaside villa of his
friends the Emperor Napoleon III and the Empress Eugenie, transformed into
a hotel in 1893.

The King's stays at Biarritz followed a regular pattern of work and pleasant
outings. Arriving by train with his staff and a small party of friends, he was
installed in his comfortable suite on the first floor of the hotel (he later moved
down to the ground floor), and the family photographs, without which he
never travelled, were arranged round the rooms. Every day the King rose at
seven o'clock, drank a glass of milk, dressed and started work on his papers
brought from London by government messengers. Breakfast was taken,
weather permitting, on the terrace outside his rooms where a tent had been set
up and the area railed round for privacy. He worked with his secretaries until
noon, and then took his daily walk before luncheon. Afternoons were devoted
to drives in his motor cars which had been brought to Biarritz by his motor
engineer and chauffeurs; picnic teas were taken in hampers – Edward himself

On 21 March 1907 King Edward drove in his motor car from Biarritz to the little village of Sare to watch the French Basque champion pelota player, Chiquito de Cambo, and his partner win a thrilling match against their Spanish Basque opponents. After the game Chiquito presented the King with a *chistera* containing a bottle of the local liqueur.
(By courtesy of the Musée Basque de Bayonne)

King Edward, near the centre of the spectators, watching the American aviation pioneer brothers, Orville and Wilbur Wright, preparing to give a demonstration flight. During the lengthy launching procedure the plane was mounted on runners and propelled along a track and into the air by the impetus of a falling weight. Wilbur flew the plane very low in front of the King, just skimming the grass.
(By kind permission of the Departmental Archives, Pau)

always drank coffee – and beauty spots and places of interest explored. Dinner was served, as were all the King's meals, in his rooms; the hotel waiters brought the dishes to the door where his own servants took them over. Friends were always invited, but the parties were small: never more than ten sat down to dinner.

Edward's methodical work routine, which he adopted wherever he travelled, seldom varied during his three weeks' stay at Biarritz. The Hôtel du Palais thus became the temporary setting for transacting British governmental business. It was to the Hôtel du Palais that the incoming Prime Minister, Herbert Asquith, was summoned in April 1908 by the King to kiss hands on assuming office. Asquith travelled by train, arrived very late on the night of 7 April, next morning had an audience, discussed his Cabinet posts and

The birth of the *Entente Cordiale*. Edward VII and French President Emile Loubet arriving at the Hôtel de Ville, Paris, on 2 May 1903.
(Bibliothèque Nationale, Paris)

lunched with the monarch, and then returned to London, while Edward went out on his usual drive. These afternoon outings were enjoyable affairs for the King, who wrote that year to a friend: 'I am very flourishing and have quite lost my cough. The sea air here and the glorious sun always agree wonderfully well with me.' The Basque countryside interested Edward, as did the local sports. He particularly liked to watch pelota, a game rather like squash played with a curved wicker racket called a chistera. And his interest in all forms of transport took him in March 1909 to the nearby town of Pau to see the Wright brothers and their flying machine.

The happiness Edward displayed on his visits to Biarritz had its roots in an event of political significance to both Britain and France: in 1903 he had managed at last to fulfil the 'dream' of which Gambetta had spoken, that of the *Entente* between the two countries. Towards the end of the century, this dream had begun to take on the qualities of a mirage, never to be realised. Britain and France were on bad terms. In 1898 antagonism caused by the 'Fashoda incident' – both countries claimed this territory in Egyptian Sudan – had been greatly exacerbated when Britain's claim was recognised; France could not forgive the withdrawal forced upon her. In the following year a war, which had been on the cards for some time, broke out between the South African Republics and Britain. France, and most of Europe, seized this opportunity to champion a small state and label Britain as aggressor. Victoria and Edward, in the forefront of the attack, were bombarded with insults, reviled and caricatured in the European press. The Prince's visits to France ceased (as did his mother's holiday trips). The Boer War dragged on, with initial defeats for the British, for almost three years. Not until 1902, with Edward then King, were the Boers brought to a satisfactory peace treaty. During all this time feelings ran high between Britain and Europe, especially France.

By the beginning of 1903 both the French and the British Government, keeping an uneasy eye on Germany, were slowly coming round to the idea of reconciliation. On his own initiative Edward determined to help this along. He proposed to take a cruise in the royal yacht, paying official calls en route on the Kings of Portugal and Italy and making stopovers at Gibraltar and Malta.

He let it be known, casually, that his homeward journey – 'quite informal' – would be overland, via Paris. The French ambassador in London heard of this and in a flurry of diplomatic activity tried to find out 'how the King wanted to be received in Paris'. Edward's confident answer – 'As officially as possible' – was conveyed to the French authorities, but what his actual reception would be was uncertain. In the meantime the cruise was turning into a triumphal progress, with the monarch rapturously received everywhere. Would Paris respond in the same way?

The critical moment arrived. On 1 May Edward stepped out of his train at the Bois de Boulogne station in Paris to be met by President Emile Loubet and state dignitaries. The carriages drove down the Champs-Elysées to the British Embassy through sullen and hostile crowds. Shouts of 'Vive les Boers!' and 'Fashoda!' and booing upset the King's suite, one of whom muttered, 'The French don't like us!', to which Edward, smiling and unperturbed, replied coolly, 'Why should they?'. After paying a ceremonial call on the President at the Elysée Palace, he addressed the British Chamber of Commerce established in Paris; in a speech which was immediately reported all over the capital he spoke warmly of his past association with France and his hope of continued friendship. That evening he went to the theatre with the President and Madame Loubet. The house was full and the atmosphere very unfriendly. In the interval Edward left his box and, strolling among the hostile audience, recognised an actress whom he had seen perform in London. With his infallible instinct for saying exactly the right thing, he smilingly took her hand and told her: 'I remember how I applauded you in London, where you personified all the grace and spirit of France.' These words buzzed round the theatre and spread like wildfire through Paris.

The official parchment signed by Edward, President Loubet and officials of the Paris Municipal Council on 2 May 1903. Edward, perhaps as a compliment to his French hosts, signed with the French version of his name: 'Edouard'. (Bibliothèque Nationale, Paris)

Next morning, smart in his Field-Marshal's uniform of red tunic, black trousers with red stripe down the side, helmet with white plumes and sporting his sash of the Légion d'honneur and French Military Medal, he rode out to Vincennes where a huge military review of some 18,000 Frenchmen under arms took place. Edward, urbane, charming and good-tempered, took the salute, punctiliously saluting the flag of every contingent as it marched past; this courtesy did not go unobserved by the watchful crowd. A big cavalcade of carriages escorted by cavalry and artillerymen then clattered back to Paris where the King was to pay a ceremonial call on the Paris Town Council at the Hôtel de Ville. Preparations there had been going on frantically all night; by nine o'clock in the morning everything was ready. Over the entrance to the Town Hall a huge awning of red velvet trimmed with gold had been erected with French and British flags in the centre. Inside the building tapestries, draperies and priceless antique vases full of flowers had been arranged. All the Town Councillors stood waiting, dressed as ordered in their uniforms or frock-coats. Outside the crowds were immense. By ten o'clock every available space was occupied; seats had been quickly put on wagons and platforms and sold to onlookers; even ladders were in demand. Spectators crammed every window along the Rue de Rivoli where the procession would pass; some clambered on to the roofs. At midday, as the cortège came dashing along, the sun, which had been obscured all morning, suddenly broke through. A huge roar of greeting burst from the crowd. As the King and President Loubet got out of their carriage, bands thundered out 'God Save the King' and 'Rule Britannia'. At the impressive and dignified ceremony Edward, in his short speech of thanks, had again chosen exactly the right words: 'I am more than delighted to be again in Paris where I always feel so much at home.' Champagne, in a beautiful Daum crystal cup, its base decorated with sea gods and mermaids as a symbolic reference to Britain's sea power, was offered to the royal visitor; a gold pen, decorated with Britain's coat-of-arms, was used by the signatories of the official parchment and, as a final dramatic touch, a messenger rushed in with a telegram bearing fraternal greetings to the Paris Town Council from the Lord Mayor and citizens of London. During the remaining two days of the visit, crammed with functions, receptions and ceremonies, the King, constantly in the public eye, was warmly applauded wherever he went. As he left Paris on 4 May 1903, shouts of 'Vive Edouard!' and 'Vive notre roi!' ('Long live *our* King!') rang in his ears.

What had caused this sudden change of heart in the Parisians? The members of Edward's suite and the diplomats in his party were unanimous in attributing it to the sheer force of his personality. The seeds of the *Entente* were already present in the changing official attitudes of the two governments. But French public opinion, especially in the capital, was still very anti-British. As the King himself had foreseen, it needed the personal appearance of one long known as a lover of France to wear down this resistance and help the *Entente* come to fruition. The Parisian crowd recognised anew their old Prince of Wales in the monarch with his beaming smile, hearty laugh, urbane and charming manners and flair for saying and doing just the right thing. The *Entente Cordiale* with France will always be associated with Edward VII, and perhaps it was the high point of his reign, a reign which opened, however, on 22 January 1901, in sorrow for the passing of the old Queen, with the anxious apprehension of Germany's future aggression and in the gloom of the prolonged Boer War.

8
FROM PRINCE TO KING

*W*HEN QUEEN VICTORIA died on 22 January 1901 her heir was aged
fifty-nine years and two months. Edward had been 'in waiting' for the
throne for almost a lifetime; his habits were established; he had settled into a
way of life; and, above all, by the wish of his mother, he had been virtually
excluded from participating in the running of the country over which he was
now called to rule. The question which the nation was asking, as the old
Queen and the old century slipped away, was: would 'The Prince' be able to
transform himself into 'The King'? The people did not have long to wait for the
answer. On the morning after his mother's death at Osborne, Edward travelled
to London to attend a meeting of the Privy Council and there take the oaths of
sovereignty. This done, the new King delivered a short address in which he
declared his intentions of following in his mother's footsteps, of being a
constitutional monarch in the strictest sense of the word, of fulfilling his
duties to the limit of his strength and – by dropping his first name of Albert –
of being known as Edward VII, thus emphasising the link with his ancestors.
This speech, on which he had consulted nobody, spontaneously delivered by
King Edward in his strong, confident voice and in his usual way without any
notes, took his listeners by surprise. It indicated a sense of responsibility, an
ability to rise to the occasion and an overnight transition to the dignities of
kingship which they had not anticipated. And the public, although still
mourning the passing of the old Queen, began to take an excited interest in
the prospect, after more than sixty years of feminine rule, of having a man in
charge – and a man, moreover, who seemed determined to tackle the duties
and responsibilities of the monarchy in a professional way. Edward had
started as he meant to go on. This was aptly illustrated on 1 February;
Victoria's coffin was conveyed from Osborne across the Solent on the Royal
Yacht *Alberta* through an avenue of ships firing a last salute and with all their
flags flying at half-mast. The King and his suite followed on the Royal Yacht
Victoria and Albert. Noticing that the flag on his ship was also at half-mast,
Edward asked the captain why. His explanation, 'The Queen is dead, Sire',
met with the terse reply 'The King lives!', and the flag shot up to the
mast-head.

Edward had inherited a country embroiled in the wearisome Boer War, and
labouring under its isolation from Europe, the result of the policy of insularity
pursued by Lord Salisbury, Victoria's last Prime Minister, whose ministry
continued under her son. (The 1867 Reform Act had abolished the regulations
which necessitated the dissolution of Parliament six months after the accession of a monarch.) Britain's foreign policy was to be the King's constant
preoccupation. But he had also inherited, from the widowed and retiring
Queen, a gloomy and restricted Court which showed few public manifestations of grandeur or dignity, and which had fallen sadly behind the times.

Edward organised the moving ceremonies of his mother's funeral at St
George's Chapel, Windsor and at Frogmore, and entertained the many royal
mourners, including Kaiser William of Germany, who came to pay their last
respects. And then on 14 February he carried out his first official function as
monarch, the State Opening of the new session of Parliament, a procedure
designed to associate the constitutional ruler directly with the country's

Edward VII, bronze cast of bust by Sydney March, 1901.
(National Portrait Gallery, London)

supreme governing body. Victoria, refusing to appear in public, had seldom performed this duty. The King determined to resume it with as much ceremonial as possible, and in addition to revive the custom of the sovereign reading the Speech from the Throne to members of both Houses assembled in the House of Lords. He gave the public the first taste of the pageantry which was to be a feature of his reign by driving in procession to Westminster. There he made a dramatic entrance through the East Door, resplendent in his uniform, red velvet state robes and shoulder cape of white ermine and carrying his white-plumed helmet. By his side Alexandra, in a black dress under her robes, sparkled with diamonds. Together they marched slowly to their Chairs of State and the King read the Speech. Henceforth the State Opening of Parliament became a regular part of Edward's expanding round of official duties.

But these functions required suitable settings, and the royal residences had been allowed to fall into a state of neglect. The monarch's London residence, Buckingham Palace, had been virtually unoccupied since Albert's death. Not only did it need cleaning, repairs and alterations, provision of bathrooms and electric light, but all the pictures and works of art had to be taken down, redistributed and rehung, and space made for Edward's private collection of pictures from Marlborough House. He decided to appoint a Surveyor and Keeper of the King's Pictures to undertake this work, and his choice fell upon Sir Lionel Cust, Director of the National Portrait Gallery in London since 1895, who had conducted him round the Gallery on a private visit on 25 February 1897. Sir Lionel began his mammoth task on 5 March 1901. While Buckingham Palace teemed with workmen gutting and restructuring the Royal apartments, cleaning and redecorating the entire building (previously gloomily nicknamed 'the sepulchre') he had all the pictures gathered in, arranged for their cleaning – many were sadly begrimed – and then set about rearranging them in the now clean and well-lit rooms. For the rehang of some particular picture he often had to consult the King, who would exclaim: 'Offer it up [i.e. put it on the wall] and I will come and see.' Bustling in cheerfully between two appointments Edward would say 'Yes' or 'No' at once, in the quick decisive manner which had become his habit. Sir Lionel acquitted himself so well that on 14 March 1902 the Palace was ready for the first Court to be held in the ballroom. Much to the satisfaction of Londoners, the Palace had again become a dignified and fitting royal residence.

Simultaneously, Windsor Castle was being 'done over'. This was a far more formidable undertaking. Victoria had made it her principal home throughout her reign. Her veneration of Albert and her dislike of change had a congealing effect on her surroundings. Albert's rooms, which would become the King's apartments, remained exactly as they had been at his death with all his possessions intact – even his medicine glass was still in place on the bedside table. As at Buckingham Palace there was little comfort and a dearth of bathrooms. During all the upheaval of spring cleaning and redecoration Sir Lionel's task at Windsor, in addition to gathering up and rearranging all the works of art, was to sift through the accumulated acquisitions of some forty years, which produced some strange finds, including dozens of plaster casts of the royal children's hands and feet, and heaps of rotting elephant tusks – a long-forgotten tribute from some African dependency. The work went on at such a smart pace that on 14 January 1902 Edward, Alexandra and the Court went into residence and stayed for a fortnight. The first dinner party was held on 26 January; the table looked lovely with a turquoise-blue Sèvres dinner service and big bowls of lilac.

The King intended Windsor Castle to fulfil its traditional role as a venue for the State visits of fellow monarchs. But he had also planned two very innovative projects. One was to open up, from time to time, the newly furbished State Apartments to the public. This democratic gesture, a practical demonstration of his determination to bridge the gulf which his mother's way of life had created between monarch and subjects, proved a huge success, with crowds turning up on the first of these occasions, Easter Day 1902. The other

Sir Lionel Cust (1859–1929), photographed in 1905. Cust was Director of the National Portrait Gallery, London from 1895 to 1909, and Surveyor and Keeper of the King's Pictures throughout Edward's reign. (National Portrait Gallery, London)

idea was to invite members of groups meeting in London – scientific congresses, learned societies, Dominion and Colonial delegations and so on – down to Windsor and show them round privately. If the King was in residence he would do the showing round himself, receiving these guests on the East Terrace if the weather were fine and indoors if wet. The tour usually ended with tea being taken in the Orangery. At other times Sir Lionel, who had been instrumental in carrying out most of the new arrangements and who had accepted the additional post of Gentleman-Usher at Court, often escorted such visitors. The first large group of this kind consisted of members of the American Chamber of Commerce whom he took round on 1 June 1902. Sir Lionel, a perceptive observer placed in a unique position to record contemporary reactions to Edward's style of kingship, noted the instantaneous success of this venture and the immense gratification of the participants. The enthusiasm never waned. Sir Lionel remembered one Canadian visitor who confided that he intended to frame, as a souvenir of the King's hospitality, the cigar offered to him after tea – Edward's smoking habits were so well known that the cigar had almost become his trade-mark. (Sir Lionel persuaded the visitor to take another cigar and smoke it there and then.)

These successful efforts to provide the new-style Edwardian monarchy with suitable settings took up relatively little of the King's time. His main preoccupations were in his preferred field of foreign policy where the first priority was to bring the unpopular and costly Boer War to an end. At his accession this conflict had been in progress for fifteen months; it was to drag on for the first year and a half of his reign, causing acute despondency at home and increasingly hostile reaction in Europe. Edward strongly supported Lord Kitchener, who had taken over from Lord Roberts as Commander-in-Chief; he urged his Ministers not to hamper him but leave decisions to the 'man-on-the-spot'; he wrote endless letters to the Secretary of State for War discussing the state of the troop reinforcements – Kitchener had complained that many of

The Boer War commanders-in-chief. (Left) Lord Frederick Roberts (1832–1914), by Inglis Sheldon-Williams, 1900; (right) Lord Horatio Kitchener (1850–1916), by C M Horsfall, 1899. (National Portrait Gallery, London)

them could not ride and knew no drill – and the poor quality of the remounts (horses) being sent out. Kitchener's rough-and-ready methods to try to combat the guerrilla tactics of the Boers, which included destroying their farms and herding their wives and children into badly run so-called 'concentration camps', aroused much indignation and provoked vociferous protests from the pro-Boer faction in Britain. But in the end Kitchener's tactics proved success-ful; by May 1902 the Boers, whose numbers in the field were dwindling, began to put out tentative feelers for peace. This eventually resolved itself into an honourable peace treaty acceptable to both sides whereby, among other conditions, the Boer Republics were incorporated into the British Empire, the Boers resettled in their homes and their farms restored, an amnesty granted to sympathisers in Cape Colony and Natal and the Dutch language given equal recognition with English in schools and law courts. The general satisfaction with the conclusion of the Boer War and with the magnanimous terms of the treaty was echoed in a personal statement published by the King on 2 June, expressing his desire for South Africa's prosperity and for the cooperation of all its inhabitants in their future welfare.

The way was now clear for King Edward's Coronation. Perhaps because of the war situation, Edward had deferred this ceremony in 1901, settling on the date of 26 June 1902. Preparations went ahead all over the country, buildings blossomed out in decorations, a jolly little jingle was being sung on the streets – 'We'll be merry, Drinking whisky, wine and sherry, Let's all be merry, On Coronation Day' – stands were erected all along the route in London and the foreign guests began arriving. These guests had been carefully selected by Edward himself. 'Crowned heads' had been ruled out because of the difficul-ties of precedence in the processions. Each ruler was asked instead to send his heir; all complied, except the Kaiser who made endless trouble and finally sent one of his brothers.

The King's timetable for June was as usual a busy one. He was due to attend a military tattoo at Aldershot on 15 and 16 June. Sir Lionel Cust, on duty at Windsor and watching him set off for this engagement, thought that he looked very ill. The weather was dreadful and he caught a bad cold; returning to the Castle, he was put to bed. On 23 June he returned to London by train. Crowds of excited onlookers cheered him as he drove out of Paddington Station with an escort of cavalry. Standing among the onlookers was the man who was to become Edward's personal motor engineer, Mr C W Stamper. He observed with anxiety that the King's eyes were closed, his head drooping and his face grey. Alexandra, sitting beside him, had to keep touching his arm gently to rouse him; each time, he struggled to raise his hat but hardly opened is eyes. That evening there was to be a grand State Dinner at Buckingham Palace for all the Coronation guests. A huge temporary banqueting hall had been built out into the garden to accommodate the suites of the royal visitors; all was bustle and excitement.

Sir Lionel, like all the Court Gentlemen-Ushers, had been detailed to meet and escort the guests arriving from abroad. His special charge was the young heir of the tiny state of Montenegro in the Balkans, Prince Danilo, whom he duly greeted at Dover and conveyed to London. Before getting on the train he learned to his dismay that the Prince, contrary to instructions, had omitted to bring his evening clothes, and that in fact he and his huge aide-de-camp had nothing to wear but their resplendent and colourful uniforms all hung about with weapons. Sir Lionel resourcefully telegraphed to a tailor whom he knew to meet the train, but travel delays unfortunately left no time to procure

London was packed with visitors from the Dominions and Colonies who had come for the Coronation, and going round the city to see the decorations became a popular outing. The magnificent Canadian Arch in Whitehall, lit up at night, attracted the sightseers and is shown here on a postcard especially produced for the occasion.
(National Portrait Gallery, London)

suitable apparel. It was only after Sir Lionel had managed to get his handsome and charming young charge to the Palace in time for the Dinner – where he provided a blaze of colour in a room of black suits – that he learned that the King was 'unwell' and would not be present. Edward, in reality, was so seriously ill that his doctors, diagnosing acute appendicitis, had warned him that if he did not undergo an immediate operation they could not answer for his life. The King, appalled at the thought of all the disappointment and disruption if the Coronation were postponed, but by then in frightful pain, finally had to agree. A room was prepared in the Palace and there, at noon on 24 June, the operation was performed. Matters had been kept so quiet, however, that the news of the operation and the postponed Coronation burst upon the public like a thunderbolt. Their reaction was similar to that of Prince Danilo. He had spent the morning driving round the capital with Sir Lionel, looking at the decorations and paying courtesy calls on members of the royal family. At one of the houses they visited they were told the dismaying news and the emotional young Prince immediately burst into tears; Sir Lionel had to escort him back to his lodgings and get him put to bed. In Westminster Abbey a dress rehearsal for the Coronation was being held; when the news erupted in the midst of these solemnities the Bishop of London had the presence of mind to turn them quickly into a service of intercession.

At the Palace the King, coming out of the anaesthetic, asked for his son George, complained about the noise of hammering – work on the Coronation stands outside the Palace was still going on – and fell into a refreshing sleep. In the Palace kitchens, however, things were not going so smoothly. News of the operation had been followed by the dismayed realisation that the great Coronation Banquet for 250 guests on 26 June would have to be cancelled. The fourteen-course menu had long before been approved by Edward. All the ingredients had been assembled – quails, legs of mutton, chickens, sturgeon, foie gras, caviare, asparagus. Many dishes had already been prepared, including sole with five garnishes, spun-sugar baskets filled with vanilla cream and jellied strawberries, and an elaborate *entrée* of snipe halved and boned, stuffed with foie gras and game forcemeat, dipped in egg and

126

breadcrumbs, grilled and served in a madeira sauce with truffles. What was to be done now with all this food? The chefs were in despair, especially as every dish in the kitchen was by this time full of jellies, some savoury ones for the cold quail, others flavoured with claret, brandy and liqueurs. The Swiss chef Tschumi had the bright idea of melting all these down and storing them in magnum champagne bottles. Two hundred and fifty bottles were soon filled and ranged along the kitchen walls. The caviare and quail were put on ice. But all the cooked food (including the snipe) and all the desserts had to be disposed of; some of the food was eaten by the staff, but the bulk was quietly taken out of the Palace and distributed by various charitable organisations for the poor to their surprised clients.

The public waited anxiously for the medical bulletins; their King showed unexpected reserves of strength and by 5 July was pronounced out of danger. The news provoked a wave of emotional loyalty, reminiscent of that after Edward's recovery from his severe illness in 1871; messages of sympathy and thanksgiving flooded in. On 15 July the King's doctors sent him on a convalescent cruise in the Solent. Although he had lost a good deal of weight he was soon his old self, strolling on the deck and writing cheerfully to his friends. His Irish nurse-in-charge, Miss Haines, was with him on board ship, staying with him for two months altogether. Edward's gratitude took the practical form of getting her appointed as Matron of the newly established Convalescent Home for Officers at Osborne (he had given this royal residence to the nation to house the Officers' Home and a Training School for Naval Cadets). The surgeon who performed the operation, Frederick Treves, was honoured with a baronetcy (the King had thoughtfully arranged this before-hand in case he did not recover).

In this joyful atmosphere a new date, 9 August, was set for the Coronation and declared a public holiday. Less than seven weeks after his operation Edward was back in London, issuing a personal message of thanks 'To My People' and preparing for the big event. This time, however, the Coronation was less of an international 'show' – the foreign royalty had gone home and most did not return – and far more of a 'family' occasion. This was especially so because of the large contingents from all parts of the British Empire. Every Dominion, Colony, Dependency and Protectorate sent representatives of the armed forces of the Crown. India had sent some of her Princes with their suites (they were invited to stay on in London to wait for the postponed Coronation), and London was crammed with Empire tourists. Before such an audience the crowning of the King, and Emperor, took on a symbolic significance and this, combined with the public's enthusiastic determination to turn the event into one of thanksgiving for the King's recovery – and for the ending of the Boer War – produced an unexpectedly festive and intimate atmosphere.

On Coronation Day huge crowds thronged the streets to cheer the coaches of Prince George and members of the royal family as they rattled past on their way to Westminster Abbey. At eleven o'clock the King's procession appeared, led by an escort of Royal Horse Guards. Then came his Bargemaster and his Watermen in their medieval costumes, his personal staff including his Indian aides-de-camp in their splendid uniforms, the Boer War heroes, Lords Kitchener and Roberts, the Yeomen of the Guard in their Tudor costumes, the King's equerries and escorts of Colonial and Indian cavalry. At last, to a great roar from the spectators, there came into sight the six superbly matched cream horses from Hanover drawing the golden and crystal coach inside which could be seen the smiling faces of Edward and Alexandra. At half-past eleven, to a joyful clamour of bells and a fanfare of trumpets, the coach drew up at the West Door. Inside the Abbey all was expectancy. After a few moments the Queen entered, escorted by the Bishops of Norwich and Oxford, with eight pages carrying her train and followed by her ladies, and she passed to her seat in the Sanctuary. Alexandra looked superb. Beneath her robes of scarlet and ermine she wore a gown of white Indian gauze, almost entirely encrusted and swagged with jewels – five separate choker necklaces, Edward's diamond and pearl wedding present necklace, the huge 'Dagmar Cross' worn as a stomacher, Victoria's sapphire brooch pinned to the bodice and her favourite serpent bracelet on her arm. Next the King's Regalia was carried in – St Edward's Crown and Staff, the Sceptres with the Cross and Dove, the Golden Spurs, the Swords, Orb and Chalice. Finally, the King entered, escorted by the Bishops of Bath and Wells and Durham; he walked firmly with no signs of weakness and to the shouts of 'Vivat Rex' from the Westminster schoolboys passed to his Chair of Recognition.

The Coronation Service began, conducted by the aged Archbishop of Canterbury, Dr Temple. Sir Lionel Cust and his wife, sitting in the South Transept Gallery, watched the impressive pageantry being recorded by the pencil of the artist, Mr Abbey, R A, tucked away on one of the Gothic tombs in the Sanctuary and drawing incessantly. They saw the Bishop of Winchester holding up large sheets of paper close to the almost blind Dr Temple to refresh his memory during the long service. The King's responses, in his deep strong voice, rang out clearly through the Abbey. When the trembling old Archbishop placed the Crown on the head of the monarch enthroned in his Coronation Chair, shouts of 'God Save the King!' echoed through the building, trumpets sounded, bells pealed and the darkness of the day was suddenly and startlingly illuminated in a blaze of electric light. The newly crowned monarch received the ceremonial acts of homage. The first to approach and kneel was Dr Temple; trying to rise he fell forward but was

King Edward VII and Queen Alexandra in their coach leaving the Abbey after the Coronation ceremony. An example of the very popular photographic postcards which documented every major event during Edward's lifetime and which were eagerly collected.
(National Portrait Gallery, London; Rotary postcard, 1902)

The Coronation of King Edward VII on 9 August 1902 in Westminster Abbey, painting by J H F Bacon, ARA. A dramatic moment depicted by the artist during the acts of homage to the crowned monarch: Edward bent forward to catch the aged Archbishop of Canterbury who fell towards him when trying to rise. (National Portrait Gallery, London)

Edward VII, painting (replica) by Sir Luke Fildes, 1902. The King invited Fildes, whose work he admired, to paint his official State Portrait and told him that probably some thirty copies would be required to send to embassies all over the world and also to fellow monarchs. While the portrait was being painted, the King chatted affably to Fildes and listened to readings from the newspapers. (National Portrait Gallery, London)

130

Alexandra, painting (replica) by Sir Luke Fildes, *c*.1893. Alexandra was delighted with Fildes' painting of her son George and Princess May after their engagement, and asked the artist to paint her own portrait. Sittings took place at Marlborough House. Alexandra wears what Fildes described as a very plain black dress, embellished by a pearl choker, pearl *sautoir* and her favourite serpent bracelet. On her knee she holds her pet Pekinese, Facey. (National Portrait Gallery, London)

(Left) Mural painting in the drawing-room at Sandringham of Alexandra, painted by Edward Hughes in 1896. The Princess wears her favourite choker necklaces of pearls, a little aigrette decoration in her swept-up hair-style, a beautiful pearl stomacher on her slim waist, and her serpent bracelet. Attached to her waist by a pearl strand is a miniature of her son Albert Victor, who died in 1892. The gaze of the Princess and her dead son address the spectator directly and thus classify this painting as a touching example of Edwardian commemorative portraiture. (Royal Collection, St James's Palace. © Her Majesty The Queen)

(Right) Mrs Langtry was asked by all the leading painters, including Millais, Leighton, Whistler and Watts, to pose for their pictures. In 1880 Edward Burne-Jones put her twice, both full-face and profile, on two of the lower steps of his *Golden Stairs*. (The Tate Gallery, London)

Sir Arthur Sullivan (1842–1900), composer,
by Sir John Everett Millais, 1888.
(National Portrait Gallery, London)

Sir Henry Irving (1838–1905), actor-
manager, by Harry Allen after Sir John
Everett Millais, c.1884.
(National Portrait Gallery, London)

Sir William Schwenk Gilbert (1836–1911), poet, dramatist and librettist of the 'Savoy' operas,
by Frank Holl, 1886.
(National Portrait Gallery, London)

Edward with his mother, father, brother Alfred and sisters watching a performance of
Shakespeare's *Macbeth* in the Rubens Room at Windsor Castle on 4 February 1853. Charles
Kean was the producer and acted in the title role; his wife Ellen played Lady Macbeth, shown
in the sleep-walking scene in this watercolour by Louis Haghe.
(Royal Library, Windsor Castle. © Her Majesty The Queen)

Ellen Terry (1847–1928),
actress, by Sir Johnston
Forbes-Robertson, 1876.
(National Portrait Gallery,
London)

Edward standing beside his father at the hunt arranged by the Emperor for his royal visitors in the Forest of St Germain, August 1855. Painting, *Imperial Hunt in the Forest of St Germain*, by Hippolyte Bellange.
(Royal Library, Windsor Castle. © Her Majesty The Queen)

Poster showing *La Goulue* dancing at the Moulin-Rouge, by Henri de Toulouse-Lautrec.
(Musée Toulouse-Lautrec, Albi)

Lord Lister (1827–1912), the pioneer of antiseptic surgery and one of the first eminent men to be awarded the Order of Merit by Edward VII in 1902. Plaster cast for wax medallion by Margaret M Giles, 1898.
(National Portrait Gallery, London)

Florence Nightingale (1820–1910), nursing and hospital reformer and the first woman to whom Edward VII awarded the Order of Merit. Pencil drawing, 1857, by Sir George Scharf, the first Director of the National Portrait Gallery in London.
(National Portrait Gallery, London)

instantly caught and supported by the King (Dr Temple died a few months later). The service ended with the crowning of the Queen, and by half-past three the carriages were driving back to the Palace through joyful crowds. That evening the Coronation banquet at last took place; there were fewer guests but the same menu. The quail came out of cold storage, the jellies were successfully melted down and re-moulded, and all the other dishes, including the delicious snipe 'cutlets', were prepared anew.

A few days later Edward emphasised the value he attached to the armed forces of the Crown by attending parades of Colonial and Indian troops in Buckingham Palace gardens, by reviewing some hundred ships of the Home Fleet at Spithead, and by admitting Lords Kitchener and Roberts to his new honour, the Order of Merit. Devised personally by the King, this prestigious Order aimed to reward outstanding achievements in the fields of science, literature, the arts and military and naval service. Membership was limited to twenty-four; Edward selected the first twelve recipients to mark his Coronation and chose Lord Lister, pioneer of antiseptic surgery, to represent science. Sir Lionel Cust was on duty at his investiture ceremony and witnessed the impressive, though somewhat embarrassing scene. Lord Lister advanced and knelt on one knee; the beautiful jewelled Order, suspended on a neck ribbon, was handed on a cushion to the King who leaned forward to bestow it. But the eminent doctor's head was too wide, or the ribbon too short, and the jewelled

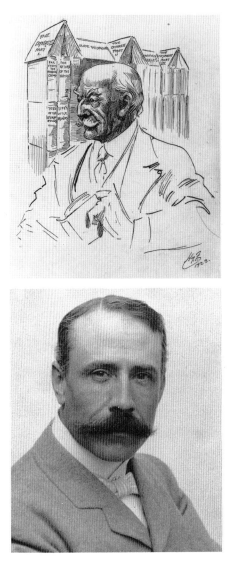

Thomas Hardy (1840–1928), novelist and poet, awarded the Order of Merit. Pen-and-ink by Harry Furniss, 1923.
(National Portrait Gallery, London)

Sir Edward Elgar (1857–1934). In March 1904 King Edward attended a three-day festival at Covent Garden devoted entirely to Elgar's music, and on 5 July of that year he conferred a knighthood on the composer. Elgar wrote his Second Symphony in E-flat for the King, but it was still incomplete when Edward died in May 1910; the pathetic slow movement is generally held to be a lament for the dead monarch to whose memory the symphony is dedicated.
(National Portrait Gallery, London; photograph by E T Holding)

Order remained poised on his nose. Edward's attempts to press it over were to no avail, and at last the recipient had to take it away in his hand, leaving the King and his suite to exchange rueful glances.

No such incidents marred the subsequent bestowals of this much-coveted Order as, over the years, the King gradually filled the vacancies. In 1907 he awarded it to Florence Nightingale, heroine of the 1854–6 Crimean War (as a twelve-year-old Edward had followed the battles of that conflict with absorbed interest and visited its wounded soldiers with his mother), tireless hospital reformer and the first woman to be thus honoured. In 1910 literature was distinguished when the writer Thomas Hardy was admitted. And music was also represented in the person of Sir Edward Elgar (although his order was not officially bestowed until after the King's death). Elgar enjoyed a friendly association with Edward, who is reported to have told him, after hearing his *Pomp and Circumstance Marches 1* and *2* in 1901, that he had written tunes which would go round the world. In 1902 Elgar was invited to compose a Coronation Ode.

King Edward VII's four prime ministers. (Top left) Robert Gascoyne-Cecil (1830–1903), 3rd Marquess of Salisbury, Conservative Prime Minister, retired in 1902. Watercolour by Sir Leslie Ward ('Spy'), c.1900. (Top right) Arthur James Balfour (1848–1930), 1st Earl of Balfour, Conservative Prime Minister 1902–5. Chalk drawing by George Richmond, 1877. (Bottom left) Sir Henry Campbell-Bannerman (1836–1908), Liberal Prime Minister 1906–8. Sanguine by Harold Speed, 1907. (Bottom right) Herbert Henry Asquith (1852–1928), 1st Earl of Oxford and Asquith, Liberal Prime Minister from 1908. Watercolour by Sir Leslie Ward ('Spy'), 1904. (National Portrait Gallery, London)

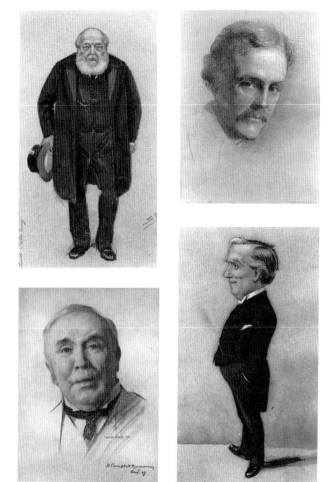

The inauguration of the Order of Merit, the restoration of the royal palaces, the regeneration of the Court, the reintroduction of pageantry, and even Elgar's exuberantly patriotic music, can all be seen as manifestations of King Edward's determination to improve Britain's prestige in the eyes of the world and to restore the country's confidence after the damaging rancour and opprobrium hurled at her during the Boer War. Britain's isolation had lasted throughout much of Victoria's reign and was the cherished foreign policy of Edward's first Conservative Prime Minister, Lord Salisbury. But times had changed and the world had moved on. Among all his Ministers, politicians and diplomats, Edward was perhaps the only man to grasp the full significance of Britain's policies in the context of the on-going European situation. His long years 'in waiting' during which he had trained himself to play the part of a 'roving ambassador' – but an 'ambassador' with little power or influence at home – had moulded his thinking and made him into one of the most knowledgeable onlookers on foreign affairs. But his opportunities to use this knowledge as King were limited. It has often been said that Edward VII never really got on to easy terms with any of his four Prime Ministers, two Conservative and two Liberal. This was partly due to differences of opinion over foreign policy and the importance accorded to it by both sides, and partly to the constantly evolving position of the 'constitutional monarch'.

Edward's reign was the first to have to come to terms with the rapid development of the main political parties, with the effect on these parties caused by the widening of the franchise (almost the whole adult male population now had the vote) and with the bitter disputes which increasingly erupted between parties and between the two Houses of Parliament. In addition, the constitutional powers of the King were far from clear; Edward found himself in the position of a monarch feeling his way through a veritable minefield of supposed past privileges as assumed by his mother, and present restrictions imposed on him by his Ministers and government departments. His first Prime Minister resigned in the weeks between his operation and his Coronation. This timing caused some surprise and provoked rumours of disagreement over foreign policy; but Salisbury was by then seventy-two years old and in failing health (he died in the following year). He nominated as his successor his nephew, Arthur Balfour, whose Conservative government lasted for the next three years. Balfour was handsome, suave, intellectual and a dedicated politician, but his airy charm was not appreciated by the King who found him annoyingly 'vague' and resented his slight but continual erosion of the royal prerogatives. Balfour's perspective of Europe differed somewhat from that of Salisbury, however, and he was more inclined to support Edward's desire to end Britain's isolation.

When Edward came to the throne Europe was split into two groupings: the Dual Alliance united France and Russia; the Triple Alliance combined Germany, Austria and Italy. Of all these countries Germany had become by far

A group photograph taken to mark the Kaiser's visit to Britain in November 1902. Back row, from left: King Edward VII, Kaiser William of Germany, Queen Alexandra, George, Prince of Wales (later George V), and Edward's second daugher, Princess Victoria; in the front row are four of Edward's grand-children: (from left) Mary, George (later George VI), Henry and Edward (later Edward VIII and Duke of Windsor).
(National Portrait Gallery, London; photograph by Lafayette)

the most powerful, the most potentially dangerous and the most vocal. Her ruler, Edward's nephew, Kaiser William, made no effort to conceal the fact that he was increasing his army and, above all, building up his navy. In spite of growing animosity between the press of both countries, Britain began to toy with the idea that friendship with Germany should be encouraged and some tentative overtures were made. Finally, after the Coronation, the King was urged to play the family card and invite the Kaiser to Sandringham for his birthday in November 1902. The King complied, but in spite of his strenuous efforts to entertain and amuse his guest the visit was not a success. It had become obvious that under a thin veneer of cordiality, suspicion and hostility still existed between the two countries and that the solution to Britain's isolation did not lie in an alliance with Germany. The Government, meanwhile, had put out feelers in an unexpected direction, towards the East. These eventually resulted in 1902 in an agreement with Japan, the terms of which, while not envisaging a full defensive alliance, yet empowered each country if need be in times of war to support each other or remain neutral; in times of peace their respective navies could work together and share facilities such as harbours and coaling stations. This Anglo-Japanese Alliance marked an historic step; it ended Britain's almost fifty years of isolation and, alongside the Dual and Triple Alliances, it introduced a third one made up of two countries whose combined navies dominated the oceans of the world.

The King, while cheerfully doing his bit – when required to do so by the Government – for the new alliance of which he thoroughly approved, by arranging for the Japanese envoys to be lavishly received and entertained, nevertheless had his eyes turned on another prospective ally – his old love France. Mutual distrust of Germany was slowly bringing the governments of Britain and her nearest European neighbour to contemplate trying to establish an understanding, but public feeling in France was still violently anti-British. The King quietly resolved to try to heal the breach himself by going to Paris, informing his ministers only after his plans had been laid. As has been seen, his visit in May 1903 turned into a resounding triumph which took both countries by surprise and which gave birth to the famous *Entente Cordiale* in 1904. The immediate result of the new understanding with France – apart from cries from Germany that she was being 'encircled' – was a flood of French official visits and delegations to Britain. First to cross the Channel was President Loubet who had received Edward in Paris. He reached London on 6 July 1903 and was put up in apartments in St James's Palace. Much thought had gone into their arrangement: Sir Lionel Cust had selected the furnishings of antiques and pictures, Edward contributed books to be laid ready for the guest. Every detail of the four-day visit was supervised by the King. For the military review at Aldershot he issued minute instructions as to what the band was to play: six bars of 'God Save the King' would do, but 'Four bars is too short' for the French national anthem; the *Marseillaise* was to be played in full. And so it was, four times in all – as the party reached the saluting base, as the contingents advanced, at the conclusion of the review and as the party left the ground. The *Marseillaise* must have enjoyed several more performances as the King escorted the President to one glittering event after another: a Gala at the opera, a State Banquet, where Edward smilingly toasted France in the Daum crystal cup presented to him in Paris's Hôtel de Ville, a visit to the State Apartments at Windsor where Sir Lionel did the honours, and a Grand Ball at Buckingham Palace. The visit was pronounced an outstanding success.

Negotiations between the governments proceeded apace, including talks on the touchy area of French and British colonial rivalry (especially strong in Egypt and Morocco). The agreement, in the form of the Anglo-French Convention Bill, was passed by the House of Commons in May, and the House of Lords in August, 1904, and was finally ratified by the French Chamber of Deputies in November of that year. Exchanges in all fields gathered momentum. In 1904 Edward lent two pictures, Clouet's *Man with a volume of Petrarch* and a panel *Scenes from the Life of St Margaret*, to an exhibition of French Primitives in Paris; Sir Lionel, as his representative, spoke of the King's love of France at the Gala luncheon and was loudly applauded. Prominent French artists, including the portrait painter Leon Bonnat and the sculptor Rodin, flocked to Windsor and had to be taken round the royal art collections, usually by Sir Lionel. In August 1905 he welcomed guests of a different type when some eighty French naval officers turned up. By this time, thanks largely to Edward's 'oiling of the wheels', the alliance was a reality, mutual suspicions between Britain and France were fading and the very term itself, *Entente Cordiale*, had entered the English language, so much so that the story went round that a Mayor, making a speech of welcome to a delegation of French municipal officers, turned frantically to a friend and whispered: 'What is the French for *Entente Cordiale*?'.

Not all the King's attention, however, was absorbed by the *Entente*. Events were rapidly moving on, both at home and abroad. At home the Boer War had revealed deficiencies in Britain's land forces; that army reform was essential was agreed by all politicians, by the public and by the King as nominal head of the army. At the same time, Britain's emergence as a world power had concentrated attention on national security and the navy, considered as the first line of defence, assumed increased importance. A Committee was set up to formulate reform, with the active participation of the King, almost the only person to have intimate detailed knowledge of the status and strength of European armies. Under Balfour's ministry army reform advanced slowly, hampered by the inevitable cries to cut service spending. Similar restrictions slowed down navy reorganisation, where the leading reformer was Admiral Sir John Fisher, a member of the Committee, Second Sea Lord in 1903, First Sea Lord in 1904 and the King's naval aide-de-camp. His spirited campaign to scrap obsolete vessels, concentrate ships in home waters to contain German aggression and above all to introduce the Dreadnought battleship into the fleet met with fierce opposition, especially from Lord Charles Beresford (Edward's former friend, Commander-in-Chief of the Mediterranean Fleet and subsequently of the Channel Fleet). The Fisher–Beresford row, with Fisher strongly supported by the King, rumbled on for years. But Fisher got his Dreadnoughts; the keel of the first of these enormous and formidably armoured vessels (with a 17,900 ton displacement, speed of 21 knots, ten 12-inch guns and twenty-six quick-firing 12-pounders) was laid down in Portsmouth in October 1905. The King launched her in February 1906; by August he and his son George (a former naval officer) were inspecting her armament and by October her steam and gun trials were under way. The Dreadnought had won her place in the fleet and two more were laid down and completed within the next two years.

Meanwhile, events abroad resulted in a tangled problem for British diplomacy. In February 1904 Japan declared war on Russia. The reasons for this were complicated and included long-standing grievances over Japanese rights in Manchuria and the independence of Korea and China. Japan, however, two days before her formal declaration, 'jumped the gun' by torpedoing two

A satirical comment in the *Punch Almanack* of 1909 on the Navy Reform row between (left) Admiral Sir John Fisher (1841–1920) and (right) Admiral Lord Charles Beresford (1846–1919).
(Reproduced by permission of *Punch*)

Russian battleships and a cruiser at Port Arthur. The repercussions of this attack resounded throughout Europe. Britain's position was a delicate one: allied to Japan, she was in honour bound either to assist or stand clear; but at the same time she was now allied to France, partner in the Duel Alliance with Russia. In addition, movements towards a better understanding between Britain and Russia had been afoot for some time. Edward, related to the Russian royal family (Czar Nicolas II was Alexandra's nephew, the Czarina was Edward's niece), trod a careful path between family feelings, British public opinion, which was in the main pro-Japanese, and the policy of his government which sought a peaceful outcome. This political line was badly shaken in October 1904 when the Russian Baltic Fleet gunned down British trawlers fishing on the Dogger Bank, sinking one and damaging others. That the Russians compounded this blunder by callously sailing on and leaving the British fishermen to drown aroused a storm of fury in Britain and violently pro-war outbursts in the press. The prompt arrival of a conciliatory personal telegram to the King from the Czar, and the Government's overriding desire to 'build bridges' with Russia prevented an immediate bellicose reaction, and Britain's injury was submitted to an independent enquiry held at The Hague. Germany now entered the equation, loudly denouncing Britain's policies as further attempts at her encirclement. The Russo-Japanese War, however, was nearing its end. In April 1905 the combined Russian fleets reached Japanese waters, only to suffer an overwhelming defeat in the Straits of Tsushima between Japan and Korea; almost all the Russian ships were sunk, damaged or taken, with huge loss of life. This crushing blow put Russia out of the war. An offer to mediate by Theodore Roosevelt, the American President, was taken up and terms of peace agreed.

With the war over, home affairs again came to the forefront; Balfour's government had fallen into difficulties. In July 1905 it was defeated on an amendment and on 4 December Balfour resigned. In the General Election early in 1906 the Conservative party lost heavily and the Liberals gained a landslide victory. When the House of Commons reassembled there were 401 Liberals, 157 Conservatives, 83 Irish Nationalists and 29 Labour members. Edward's first Liberal Prime Minister was Sir Henry Campbell-Bannerman; he brought into government new men – Herbert Asquith as Chancellor of the Exchequer and David Lloyd George as President of the Board of Trade – who were to have a profound influence on British politics for the remainder of the King's reign. The dynamic Lloyd George, representing the Liberal radical wing, galvanised his bureaucratic department. He pushed through the hotly contested Old Age Pension (five shillings a week) and proposed insurance schemes, thus laying the foundation for the modern Welfare State (in all this he was copying Bismarck who had started state benefits in Germany in the 1880s). Edward had no particular liking for Lloyd George, but he contrived to get on reasonably well with most of the other Liberals. John Burns, the working-class man who

David Lloyd-George (1863–1945), 1st Earl,
Liberal politician. Pencil and wash by Sir
Max Beerbohm, *c*.1908.
(National Portrait Gallery, London)

Sir Winston Spencer Churchill (1874–1965)
in the uniform of the Lancashire Hussars.
(National Portrait Gallery, London)

became President of the Local Government Board, is reputed to have re-
marked: 'Me and 'im get on first-rate together.' Another of the 'new men' was
Winston Churchill, given the post of Under-Secretary of State for the Colonies.
The King had for long been acquainted with the family of this young man who
had already contrived to bring himself to the notice of the public. Having
served with the British Army in India and the Sudan, he went out to the Boer
War in October 1899 as a war correspondent for a London newspaper.
Captured by the Boers, he made a daring escape and returned home a hero. He
began his Parliamentary career in 1900 as a Conservative, changed over to the
Liberals in 1904 and held office throughout Edward's reign. The King was
sometimes irritated by Winston's impetuous outpourings, but he remained on

friendly and sociable terms with him. Writing to a friend from Biarritz in 1907 he mentioned that Admiral Fisher and Winston had come to visit him and that they were most amusing together, adding ironically that he dubbed this pair 'the chatterers'.

Campbell-Bannerman's leadership of the Liberal Government lasted for only two years. Early in April 1908 the Prime Minister, five years older than Edward and in failing health, had to resign (he died two weeks later). His place was taken by Herbert Asquith, Lloyd George became Chancellor of the Exchequer and Winston Churchill President of the Board of Trade. Although Campbell-Bannerman had often annoyed the King by failing to keep him fully informed on political matters, he had gradually become his friend and possibly his most congenial Prime Minister. The two men had many tastes and interests in common. To Campbell-Bannerman Edward could write bracingly and kindly, suggesting as remedies for a bout of ill-health 'a glass or two of champagne' and a few days' rest in the healthy air of Balmoral – both remedies were gratefully accepted. The King was never to get on such easy terms with the reserved Asquith, and even less so with Lloyd George. But with one Liberal Minister, Robert Haldane, Secretary of State for War, he did form a fruitful relationship. Under Balfour's government the movement for army reform had come up against financial resistance, and Haldane had to fight the same reluctance in the Liberal administration to spend money on the services. But both he and the King realised that for Britain to hold her own on the Continent in the event of war she must have an efficient fighting-machine and that probably this should consist of a highly trained strike force, backed up by a Territorial Army reserve. Haldane, helped by Edward to the utmost of his influence, eventually got his well-equipped British Expeditionary Force of 120,000 men made up of one cavalry and six infantry divisions (a number which appeared derisory to European countries with their huge conscripted armies). As for the Territorials, the King was tireless in encouraging this venture, receiving the officers of newly formed units, presenting colours and reviewing troops all over the country. In the course of all this joint activity, the King and his Secretary of State for War, although they sometimes had differences of opinion, became friends. When Haldane visited Edward at Marienbad where he was taking the 'cure' and drinking the waters, their long discussions on army reform were punctuated by sociable outings in the King's motor car and picnics in the woods.

As King, Edward could, and in fact did, conduct state business anywhere he happened to be. His routine of travelling, contrary to some expectations, had in no way been curtailed on his accession to the throne. His journeyings, both abroad and at home, had if anything been increased, due largely to the motor car. As Prince, Edward had already taken rides in friends' cars, and his approval of this form of transport ensured its popularity. He was entreated to help industry by including a 'motor coach' in his Coronation procession, but this idea was dropped because of the problems of vibration and noise. He did, however, patronise the Automobile Exhibition, add 'Royal' to the Automobile Club's title and acquire his own fleet of cars, all painted claret colour, with blue leather upholstery, the Royal Arms on the doors and no number-plates. Together with his cars the King acquired the very necessary services of his motor engineer, Mr C W Stamper. The latter's accounts of some of the hair-raising excursions he enjoyed with the King, getting stuck on steep hills and in muddy fields or deluged with rain, aptly illustrate the exciting days of early motoring. He sat beside the chauffeur on the front seat and if anything

King Edward VII's 1900 Daimler Tonneau.
(National Motor Museum, Beaulieu)

went wrong with the car – and it often did – his job was to put it right. This usually entailed changing the wheel, a lengthy operation. But at other times literally 'running repairs' were effected, with the vehicle chugging along and Stamper crawling over the bonnet, lying on the wings or standing on the running-board keeping the King informed of progress. The motor car became part of Edward's public image. Both on the Continent, where his cars were waiting when he stepped off the train, and at home, crowds of onlookers grew accustomed to seeing the big car driving by with the King sitting inside smiling and lifting his hat. And on country roads they also got used to hearing him shout 'Blow your horn, Stamper!' as the car neared some obstacle, followed by the clarion-call of the four-key bugle specially purchased for this purpose.

Everything the King did was of interest. He was always in the public eye, and often literally so, since many of his activities, such as going to the races, were shared by masses of his subjects; in 1900 Edward had an amazing run of successes as an owner. As King he still attended all the big race meetings, where he was always affectionately greeted with shouts of 'Good old Teddy!'. But his horses were disappointing until Derby Day, 26 May, 1909. His runner, Minoru, was in top form and highly fancied. Huge crowds flocked to Epsom hoping to see something which had never happened before, namely a reigning sovereign win this prestigious event. Minoru was drawn badly, on the inside; but his jockey got him smartly away and well placed at the front of the field, where the colt liked to race, just behind the two pace-makers. The excitement was tremendous as the horses swept round Tattenham Corner at a cracking pace with Minoru on the rails. With his long striding gallop, Minoru, almost neck and neck with a challenger, carried the King's colours past the winning post. Pandemonium broke out when the announcement came that Edward's horse had won. The beaming King, struggling down from the stands to lead in his champion, was almost submerged in the frantically cheering crowds; hats and even policemen's helmets were thrown in the air; shouts of 'Good old Teddy!' merged with lusty singing of 'God Save the King' which rang through all the enclosures and far down the course.

Such scenes had never been witnessed before. They were widely reported in

King Edward VII at Epsom for the Derby, 26 May 1909, with a group of friends, including his stable manager, Lord Marcus Beresford (immediately to right of the King) and his son George.
(National Portrait Gallery, London; photograph by William Booty)

the newspapers which were now a part of daily life and had become a powerful factor in moulding public opinion. Recurrent war scares and fears of German invasion were fostered largely through this medium. The King's actions abroad were closely monitored for any revealing indications of Britain's policy. When Edward and Campbell-Bannerman happened to be taking the 'cure' at Marienbad Spa at the same time, a photograph showing them in close conversation was published with the caption 'Is it Peace or War?', and little notice was taken of the Prime Minister's solemn disclaimer (though possibly delivered with a twinkle in his eye) that the King had only asked his opinion on a culinary matter as to whether halibut tasted better boiled or baked. An ominous shadow was indeed creeping over Britain's domestic policies and foreign affairs. Edward's happy Derby Day was only an oasis in an increasingly worrying situation for the constitutional monarch he had pledged himself to be.

In 1909 Britain appeared to have manoeuvred herself into a strong position abroad. Her diplomatic isolation was a thing of the past. Her alliances with Japan and France remained intact and to them in 1907 she had added an agreement with Russia – in spite of strong doubts expressed on the Czar's repressive regime – which settled areas of dispute regarding Persia, Afghanistan and Tibet. In addition, her relations with Spain, Portugal and the Scandinavian countries were free from friction. All this, however, had the unhappy effect of alienating Germany, who reiterated her accusations of 'encirclement' and whose Kaiser alternated between fulsome expressions of friendship for Britain and fulminations against his uncle for what he termed his Machiavellian cunning. Attempts had been made by successive British governments to conciliate the Kaiser with the help of the King. Edward had been urged to meet his nephew on occasions both formal and informal; he had paid a State Visit to Kiel in 1904, had invited the Kaiser on a return State Visit to Windsor in 1907, and in February 1909 Asquith requested him to pay a three-day State Visit to Berlin. A crowded schedule of functions was arranged. The King, suffering from his customary bronchial trouble, was hard put to get through it, and had one bad attack of coughing and choking which alarmed his fellow-guests at a luncheon (recovering quickly, he immediately lit a large cigar). Edward scored a personal triumph in Berlin. The populace, at first cool, was soon responding warmly to his dignified ease of manner, affability and charm. But the change of heart was only momentary and the underlying hostility remained. The King realised this and issued a sombre warning to the Government when he wrote to Asquith at the beginning of May foretelling, for the first time, the possibility of a European war.

While war-clouds were gathering abroad, domestic problems were looming large on the home front. The 'People's Budget', introduced by Lloyd George in spring 1909, started the row and brought about the constitutional crisis which was still unresolved at Edward's death a year later. The Government had been forced to bow to public demand to bring the navy up to a strength equal, or superior, to the German fleet. To pay for this, and for the new welfare benefits, Lloyd George proposed to increase income tax and impose other duties and taxes on the upper classes. On 5 November 1909 his Budget was passed by a large majority in the House of Commons; it was then sent to the House of Lords who promptly threw it out. A titanic clash between the two Houses, shaking the constitutional foundations of government, now ensued. The Commons' case was that the Lords were blocking their democratic rights fought for throughout British history; the Lords, while stoutly defending their hereditary privileges, declared that such radical measures could only be decided by the whole country at a General Election. The King, in the thick of the struggle, vainly attempting to bring the two angry antagonists to conciliation, had to try to define the unclear limits of the power and influence of a constitutional monarch. He held in his hand the royal prerogative of forcing the Lords to pass the Bill by creating enough new Liberal peers to ensure a majority, but the number to be created would be enormous – more than 300. The King knew that if he did this the prerogative would pass from himself – and from his heirs – to the Government, and that there would be nothing to stop the next government in power from following this precedent. Events moved on inexorably. Parliament was dissolved in December 1909 and a bitter campaign, fought on the right of the House of Lords to reject a Finance Bill, preceded the General Election of January 1910. In the newly elected House of Commons the Liberals had lost so many seats that they and the Conservatives were almost equal, with 275 and 273 seats respectively; Labour seats had increased to 43, the Irish Nationalists remained around 80. The crisis had, if anything, worsened. The King invited Asquith to Windsor to discuss the situation. To his amazement the Prime Minister, violating all the rules of etiquette, declined, giving the somewhat weak excuse that he was 'done up' and had to go abroad to Cannes for a holiday. On 22 February Edward performed the State Opening of Parliament and in his Speech referred to the still unresolved question of relations between the two Houses. Asquith was determined to get the Budget through the Commons again before bringing up

King Edward VII and Queen Alexandra in their State Robes for the Opening of Parliament.
(National Portrait Gallery, London; photograph by W and D Downey)

the issue of the Lords and their veto.

The problem of his own line of action was still weighing heavily on the mind of the King, who was perhaps more in need of a holiday than his Prime Minister. Such was the opinion of his doctors, worried by his weakened condition and alarmed by his frequent and violent attacks of bronchial coughing. They finally got him away from the London fog on 7 March. That evening in Paris he went to the theatre; the building was over-heated and he caught a chill. By the time he got to Biarritz he was in the throes of a severe

Postcard photograph of Edward VII with Caesar, his favourite dog, whose collar bore the inscription: 'I belong to the King'. Caesar was passionately devoted to his master, went everywhere with him, travelling by train, sitting on the back seat of the car, and accompanying him on walks. On these outings Caesar would often dash off to hunt. The whole party would have to shout and whistle for him, and Caesar would eventually turn up with such an innocent air that no one, least of all the King, could ever be angry with him. (National Portrait Gallery, London; photograph by T H Voigt)

attack of bronchitis and remained indoors in his suite at the Hôtel du Palais. When he failed to appear at church on Sunday 13 March, rumours flew round the town that he was very ill. None of this was reported in the English newspapers, although a nurse, Miss Fletcher, was sent out from England. Not until 21 March did Edward leave the hotel, on a short outing for luncheon. By 8 April he was better, working on his papers every morning, taking his usual excursions with friends in his motor car through the countryside in the afternoons, and strolling on the promenade with his favourite dog, the perky and mischievous little fox terrier Caesar. He found time to present the town of Biarritz with a horse-drawn ambulance, sending his nurse, Miss Fletcher, to supervise the arrangements. And the town responded by organising a municipal send-off on his last evening, a jolly and noisy affair with fireworks, illuminations and a great procession of soldiers, sailors and military bands marching past the King who waved and saluted from his hotel balcony. On the following day, 26 April, he set off back to London and the unresolved crisis, burdened with the worry of his forthcoming decision and with his intuitive feelings that domestic political squabbles were obscuring the real dangers of a European war.

Outwardly calm and cheerful as he visited the opera and the Royal Academy and held audiences, he was still far from well. On Saturday 30 April Edward went to his beloved Sandringham for the weekend; the weather was very cold, but on that day and again on Sunday he insisted on touring the estate, visiting the gardens and stables and discussing improvements with his staff, and in doing so had a recurrence of his bronchitis. When the King returned to Buckingham Palace on Monday 2 May his doctors advised rest; he shrugged off this advice and continued to work. But he could not sleep and could hardly speak for prolonged bouts of coughing and choking. Alarm about his condition began to spread through the Palace, but the public was not informed. Edward continued to get up, dress himself sprucely in his formal attire of frock-coat, and receive visitors, but his condition was obviously deteriorating. Queen Alexandra, cruising in the Mediterranean, was hastily sent for; she arrived in London on the evening of 5 May. That the King was not at the railway station to meet her, as was his custom, aroused panic in the onlookers. A medical bulletin, which Edward drafted in his own hand, was therefore issued to the effect that the King was suffering from bronchitis and that his condition was causing some anxiety.

On the morning of 6 May Edward insisted on getting up. Surrounded by the worried faces of his son George, his wife, entourage and doctors, he alone was calm and cheerful. Declaring 'I shall not give in', he received his old friends, sitting up fully dressed in his chair and steadfastly refusing to be put to bed. Between recurring heart attacks and moments of faintness, he smiled on being told that his horse, Witch of the Air, had won her race at Kempton Park that afternoon. That the King had wanted his horse to run, and that she had won, was at first taken by the public as a kind of hopeful omen of his recovery. But nothing emerged from the Palace to support this optimism and anxious crowds began to gather at the Palace gates. The King was sinking, knowing that he was dying, but his last words were a brave declaration of his love of life: 'No, I shall not give in; I shall go on; I shall work to the end.' At half-past eleven he lost consciousness and was placed on his bed. And at a quarter-to-midnight he slipped away.

9

THE END OF A KING AND OF AN AGE

'*THE KING* is dead.' When this message was brought down at midnight on 6 May 1910 to the crowds waiting at the gates of Buckingham Palace it was received in a stunned silence of disbelief. Next morning the country woke to the realisation that their 'Good old Teddy' had gone. The sense of personal loss was extraordinarily widespread. Edward's reign had lasted for only nine years, but during all his long life 'in waiting' he had been the public's 'Roaring Royal Boy'. By the time he came to the throne thousands of his subjects had sat with him through church services and concerts, through performances in the theatre and opera house, had strolled with him on race courses, had watched him opening hospitals, libraries, exhibitions, laying foundation stones, driving through their streets courteously lifting his hat, smiling his good-natured smile, smoking his cigar. Thousands more had shaken his hand, seen the twinkle in his beaming blue eyes, heard his chuckling, rumbling laugh. The image of the Edwardian King had been firmly stamped on the public consciousness long before he came to the throne, an image which combined regal dignity with jovial humanity. The disappearance of his huge exuberant personality brought to many the feeling of a void which his son George, the new King George V, sadly expressed in his diary as the loss of his 'best friend and the best of fathers'.

As the church bells, which sixty-eight years before had jubilantly rung in his birth, and a mere seven years ago his Coronation, began their sombre tolling all over the country, tributes to the dead King poured in, and not only from the monarchies. Republican America's House of Representatives, after passing a vote of sympathy, adjourned as a mark of respect; New York, where

The lying-in-state at Westminster Hall. This photograph, and the four following, are examples of the picture postcards on sale to the public after the funeral of Edward VII. (National Portrait Gallery, London)

the young Prince had whirled so happily round the dance floor long ago, suspended business on its Stock Exchange for the day, flew its flags at half-mast and played 'God Save the King' in its theatres.

The King's body lay in state in the Throne Room in Buckingham Palace. All the leading politicians, members of his household and old friends were invited to make their private farewells. On 17 May the coffin was taken to Westminster Hall for the three-day public Lying-in-State. Silent crowds watched and bands played funeral marches as the procession made its slow way through St James's Park, along the Mall and up Whitehall. In the dimly lit Hall the coffin was placed on a huge bier; around it stood, immobile and with bowed head, officers of the British and Indian Armies. During the three days of the vigil a steady stream of members of the public – the number was estimated at 250,000 – passed silently and reverently through the Hall. Entering by the steps at the south end, they passed by slowly on each side of the bier, pausing to pay their last respects – many of the women curtsied, and men bowed – before leaving by the big doors into Palace Yard. Foreign royalties arriving for the funeral joined the mourners in Westminster Hall – the Kings of Portugal, Spain, Belgium, Bulgaria, Greece, Norway and Denmark, the Kaiser clasping the hand of his cousin, the new King George V, and, among some thirty royal princes, the deeply moved Prince Danilo of Montenegro, again in the charge of Sir Lionel Cust.

On the morning of 20 May preparations for the funeral began early. By eight o'clock the courtyard at Buckingham Palace was full of long lines of saddled and bridled horses held by their grooms, all standing ready for the royal mourners who were to ride in the procession from Buckingham Palace to Westminster Hall and on to Paddington Station. At last the signal to mount was given and the cortège set off, the horsemen followed by carriages containing the royal ladies and their suites. At Westminster Hall the coffin was placed on a gun-carriage and the long procession re-formed. The coffin was followed by two grooms leading the late King's favourite charger; the saddle

The funeral procession winds its way through packed crowds in Windsor. On arrival at Windsor the gun-carriage was drawn by sailors, and the royal mourners went on foot. Postcard photograph.
(National Portrait Gallery, London)

Queen Alexandra, the Queen Mother, heavily veiled, riding in one of the royal coaches following the mounted mourners. Postcard photograph. (National Portrait Gallery, London)

The King's Funeral. Queen Alexandra. The most pathetic figure in the Procession. (9)

was empty and his boots reversed in the stirrups. Immediately behind trotted Caesar, led by one of the late King's loaders in Highland dress. The sight of the anxious little dog still looking for his master brought tears to the eyes of many in the hushed crowd. With the rumble of wheels, creaking of harness and clatter of horses' hooves, the slow procession moved through streets funereally draped in purple and white and lined with servicemen standing with arms reversed. At Paddington the coffin was entrained and conveyed to Windsor, where the procession re-formed to proceed on foot, with the gun-carriage drawn by lines of sailors, through the streets of the town and down the Long Walk to St George's Chapel. Here, where Edward had married Alexandra forty-seven years before, he was finally laid to rest.

Thus ended, amid widespread grief, the reign so long awaited and so short in duration, of Edward VII, one of the best-known and most popular of British Kings. Even over a gulf of eighty years and in a world far removed from that of the Edwardian Age, his image is still a familiar one – elegantly dressed, portly, nonchalant, smiling, waving his cigar, affable, kind and dignified. What were the qualities which turned him into a King 'Beloved of his People', and what were the achievements of his reign?

In 1860 the young Prince of Wales came back from his trip to the New World a changed man. His wildly successful public appearances had restored the self-confidence which his schooling had all but destroyed. Almost overnight,

In the procession, immediately after the late King's charger and Caesar, rode the new King George V (centre), escorted by King Edward's only surviving brother Arthur, Duke of Connaught (far left), and Edward's nephew the Emperor of Germany (Kaiser William) on a white horse (foreground). (National Portrait Gallery, London)

he had matured, learned how to deliver a speech, how to listen, how to deal with the unexpected, how to adapt himself to any company. (None of this was particularly appreciated by his parents; Victoria was inclined to dismiss public appearances as irrelevant, and Albert was engrossed in educational plans.) But Edward had understood his profession and had started to train himself to be a King. That almost six-sevenths of his life was spent in this training and only one-seventh in actual practice is one of the ironies of Fate, for whom crowned heads possess no privileges. This particular crowned head may have privately railed at the unfairness both of life and of his mother who denied him a share in political affairs; but Edward had the grace and good manners never to criticise in public, never to form a rival 'Court', never to undermine his mother's dignity.

This painfully acquired experience, however, served to mould his behaviour towards his own heir. Edward VII's relations with his son George were more than exemplary; he tried to train and guide him for his future role, and did it all with love. Contemporaries described their relationship as more like that of affectionate brothers than that of father and son (Edward was only twenty-three when George was born). When Edward died, George declared that he had never had a cross word with him in his life. And Edward ran counter to his mother's dictum of using her family as political pawns in arranged marriages, by allowing his daughters to choose their own husbands. (As for

The Archbishops receiving the coffin at St George's Chapel, Windsor. As the bearers prepare to carry the coffin into the chapel, all stand at the salute, the guards in the foreground with their arms reversed.
(National Portrait Gallery, London)

his boys, when his then heir, Albert Victor, fell head-over-heels in love with a Roman Catholic princess whose father was pretender to the French throne, Edward was even willing, for the sake of his son's happiness, to consider an alliance which would have caused immense religious, and political, difficulties.)

Many reproaches were directed at Edward, by his contemporaries and by later critics, for his apparent self-indulgence – his shooting parties, his houses full of servants, his stables full of horses, his grand dinners, his weekend house parties, his lady friends, his 'scrapes', his constant travelling. Edward of course was only following a lifestyle common to the aristocracy and upper classes all over Europe. But he improved on the Continental model by stamping his unique elegance and flair on his Edwardian Society and, more importantly, by throwing open its doors to men of the arts and professions. And it soon became apparent to the Edwardian public – as it has recently been recognised – that Edward's pursuit of pleasure never obscured his real sense of duty. And it might be added that his routine of regular work hours, his punctuality and attention to detail, remarked upon by all around him when he became King, could not have been acquired suddenly at the age of fifty-nine but rather represented the self-discipline of a lifetime.

What did Edward achieve in his short reign? At home he inherited a country still locked in the caste-like class system in which one-third of the population below the poverty line struggled to keep alive in mean little slum houses, with long hours of work in unhealthy condtions and not enough food. Was Edward interested in social reform? Perhaps, perhaps not. (He certainly could not abide the Suffragettes; like most Edwardian men he preferred women to be elegant and amusing, or quietly domestic, although he did approve of those who performed the 'womanly' tasks of nursing and social work.) His views were in the main still those of the Victorians; he believed in providing libraries, museums, exhibitions, so that the working classes could educate themselves, and he worked energetically all his life to provide these adjuncts to 'self-help'. However, it was after all in his reign that the foundations of the Welfare State were firmly laid, when Lloyd George introduced the Old Age Pension. The King did nothing to assist this very necessary and humanitarian innovation. On the other hand, he did nothing to prevent it. His comment was far removed from the horrified upper-class denunciations of this measure to the effect that poor old men with five shillings in their hand would spend it all on riotous living, but rather questioned whether enough money would be left to pay for Britain's defence in the war which he saw only too clearly to be imminent. And this observation confirms what everyone, including the public, saw as Edward's main interest and preoccupation – foreign affairs. To subscribe to the view of some of Edward's Continental contemporaries that he was an international manipulator of Machiavellian proportions, carrying out grandiose schemes and acting with full powers all his life, is as damaging to his reputation as is the notion that he merely jauntered round Europe enjoying himself. His statesmanship and diplomacy were recognised early on by Disraeli but remained largely unused. But with very little power, and not much encouragement, he yet achieved much – urging Britain out of her isolation, upholding her prestige, intuitively finding exactly the right moment to bring about the *Entente Cordiale*, getting up the strength of the country's defences while constantly striving for peace. A popular cockney ditty sung in the music halls:

> There'll be no wo'ar
> As long as there's a King like good King Edward
> There'll be no wo'ar
> For 'e 'ates that sort of thing!
> Mothers needn't worry
> As long as we've a King like good King Edward
> Peace with 'Onner
> Is his Motter
> So God Sive the King!

sums up the public's faith in their 'Good old Teddy', in his role as 'King Edward the Peacemaker', to interpose his majestic bulk between them and any horrors poised to fall on them.

The public had long recognised the essential element in Edward, that as well as being a 'Royal' he was a human being like themselves, with the same joys and sorrows, pleasures and pains, strengths and weaknesses. Perhaps the greatest and most enduring achievement of Edward VII, whose image is indelibly stamped on the pages of history, was that he 'humanised' the monarchy.

Beloved of his People: His Late Majesty King Edward VII. This photograph by Baron de Meyer was issued to commemorate Edward's death.
(National Portrait Gallery, London)

SELECT BIBLIOGRAPHY

*A*MONG ALL the books written on Edward VII and the Edwardian Age the two huge volumes of Sir Sidney Lee's official biography, *Edward VII* (Macmillan, 1925, 1927) still hold pride of place, with an in-depth analysis of the political situation throughout Edward's life and an invaluable mass of information not readily available elsewhere. Among later works, the best short biography is Roger Fulford's excellent, and unbiased, chapter on Edward VII in his volume *Hanover to Windsor: British Monarchs from 1830–1936* (Fontana/ Collins, 1960); Catherine Gavin's *Edward VII: A Biography* (1941) is particularly good on Franco-British relationships during the reign, and other fairly recent studies include those by Sir Philip Magnus, *King Edward the Seventh* (John Murray, 1964), Keith Middlemas, *The Life and Times of Edward VII* (Weidenfeld and Nicolson, 1972) and Christopher Hibbert, *Edward VII: A Portrait* (Allen Lane, 1976).

Contemporary accounts of some of Edward's activities include his trip to the New World chronicled by Kinahan Cornwallis, *Royalty in the New World or the Prince of Wales in America* (1860), and by Nicholas Augustus Woods, correspondent of *The Times*, *The Prince of Wales in Canada and the United States* (1861). Another *Times* correspondent, W H Russell, 'covered' the Prince's wedding, *A memorial of the marriage of H.R.H. Albert Edward, Prince of Wales and H.R.H. Princess Alexandra* (Day and Son, 1863), and after accompanying him to India in 1875–6, wrote an account of that trip, *The Prince of Wales' Tour of India: a diary with some account of the visits of H.R.H.* (1877), illustrated by the artist who was also on the tour, Sydney Prior Hall.

After Edward's death many of those who had come into contact with him in various ways published their reminiscences. Outstanding in this field are the memoirs of Sir Lionel Cust (former Director of London's National Portrait Gallery), *Edward VII and his Court* (John Murray, 1930), a witty, informative and perceptive view of the King. C W Stamper's *What I know: Reminiscences of five years' personal attention upon King Edward the Seventh* (Mills and Boon, 1913), goes far to explain Edward's ability to charm; Xavier Paoli's *My Royal Clients* (Hodder and Stoughton, 1911) provides an interesting comparison between security measures for the Royals then and now, and Gabriel Tschumi's *Royal Chef: Recollections of Life in Royal Households* (William Kimber, 1954) transports the reader behind the scenes into the hot and bustling kitchens. As for the ladies in Edward's life, Mrs Lillie Langtry wrote her own memoirs, *The Days I Knew* (1925), while Mrs Alice Keppel's daughter, Sonia, contributes a delightful account of her mother in *Edwardian Daughter* (Hamish Hamilton, 1958).

The Edwardian Age has received its full quota of literary offerings. Among these may be singled out Barbara Tuchman's *The Proud Tower: A portrait of the world before the War, 1890–1914* (1962, Macmillan, 1980), in which she holds a magnifying glass to twenty-four vital years of European history, which included Edward's reign, leading up to the First World War. In a lighter vein, Pauline Stevenson provides a mass of detail on *Edwardian Fashion* (Ian Allen, 1980), as does Suzy Menkes on *The Royal Jewels* (1985). Easily the best overall view is to be found in J B Priestley's *The Edwardians* (Heinemann, 1970), an invaluable reference book on the theatrical, artistic, literary and social life of the period and which also contains a thoughtful analysis of Edward himself.

How Edward's image was diffused can be found in the relevant contemporary issues of the *Illustrated London News* which kept the public informed of all the main events of his life in pictures – and prose – while a satirical eye was cast over the whole of the same period by *Punch* magazine, born in the same year as Edward, as was, to all intents and purposes, photography. The catalogue by Malcolm Rogers of the exhibition *Camera Portraits: Photographs from the National Portrait Gallery 1839–1989* (NPG Publications, 1989) chronicles the early days of this new art form. London's National Portrait Gallery contains a unique and comprehensive collection of 'Edwardian faces', all fully documented – together with the rest of the collection – in the *National Portrait Gallery Complete Illustrated Catalogue*, compiled by K K Yung (1980).